STANDARDS EXEMPLAR SERIES

Assessing
Student Performance
Grades K–5

NCTE Executive Committee

President Carol Avery
President-Elect Sheridan Blau
Vice President Joan Naomi Steiner
Past President Beverly Ann Chin
Representatives-at-Large Diane T. Orchard, Greta D. Price, Richard Luckert
Elementary Section Chair Pat Cordeiro
Secondary Section Chair Carolyn Lott
Secondary Section Associate Chairs Kay Parks Bushman, Charleen Silva Delfino
College Section Chair Frank Madden
College Section Assistant Chair Gail E. Hawisher
CCCC Chair Nell Ann Pickett
CEE Chair Richard K. Harmston
CEL Chair Mary Ellen Thornton
Executive Director Faith Z. Schullstrom
Deputy Executive Director Charles Suhor
Associate Executive Director Karen Smith
Associate Executive Director for Higher Education Gesa E. Kirsch

Advisory Groups for the K–5 Book

Project Share Teachers from Columbus, Ohio

Brenda Doyle
Linda Gore
Christine Ault
Ashley Lenhart
Sharon Dorsey
Jan Higdon

Teachers from Northern Elementary School, Fayette County Public Schools, Lexington, Kentucky

Michelle Dickson
Sara Anderson
Michelle Murphy

STANDARDS EXEMPLAR SERIES

Assessing Student Performance Grades K–5

Edited by

Miles Myers
and Elizabeth Spalding

National Council of Teachers of English
1111 W. Kenyon Road, Urbana, IL 61801-1096

Grateful acknowledgment is made to the following authors, publishers, and agencies for permission to use materials from their works:

Pages viii–xix, 44–47, and 54–61: From *NAEP 1992 Writing Report Card,* by Arthur N. Applebee, Judith A. Langer, Ina V. S. Mullis, Andrew S. Latham, and Claudia A. Gentile (Report No. 23-W01, June 1994); *Reading Assessment Redesigned: Authentic Texts and Innovative Instruments in NAEP's 1992 Survey,* by Judith A. Langer, Jay R. Campbell, Susan B. Neumann, Ina V. S. Mullis, Hilary R. Persky, and Patricia L. Donahue (Report No. 23-FR-07, January 1995); *Trends in Academic Progress,* by Ina V. S. Mullis, John A. Dossey, Mary Foerth, Lee R. Jones, and Claudia Gentile (NAEP and the Educational Testing Service, 1991); and *Reading Framework for the 1992 National Assessment of Educational Progress* (NAGB 92-5002). NAEP is a congressionally mandated project of the National Center for Education Statistics of the U.S. Department of Education. NAEP reports are prepared for the Office of Educational Research and Improvement of the U.S. Department of Education by the Educational Testing Service, Princeton, New Jersey, under contract with the National Center for Education Statistics.

Pages 7 and 9: From a spelling lexicon by Susan Sowers. Reprinted by permission of Donald Graves, *Writing: Teachers and Children at Work* (Heinemann, a division of Greenwood Publishing Group, Portsmouth, NH, 1983).

Pages 8 and 9: From "How Do You Spell Caught?" reprinted in *The Quarterly of the National Writing Project* 17 (4), Fall 1995. Reprinted with permission of the Pennsylvania Writing Project/West Chester University.

Page 10: From "Emily: A Case Study," by Judie Bartch, *Primary Voices K–6* 4 (4), November 1996. Copyright © 1996 by NCTE.

Page 11: From "I Do Teach and the Kids Do Learn," by Wendy J. Hood, *Primary Voices K–6* 3 (4), November 1995. Copyright © 1995 by NCTE.

Pages 18 and 19: From "The Tattler's Tales: Some Authentic Writing Samples from Six-Year-Olds," *The Quarterly of the National Writing Project* 18 (2), Spring 1996. Reprinted with permission.

Pages 20–24: From *The San Mateo Writing Project,* 1979, a study by M. Myers, J. Grahem, and L. Williams. Reprinted with permission.

Pages 33–36 and 62–77: From *A Sampler of English-Language Arts Assessment: Elementary.* Copyright © 1994 by the California Department of Education. Reprinted with permission.

Pages 48–53: From *Toolkit: Evaluating the Development and Implementation of Standards.* Copyright © 1997 by the Council of Chief State School Officers, Washington, D.C. All rights reserved with the exception of reproduction for educational purposes.

Pages 78–83: From *New Standards 1994–95 Portfolio Field Trial.* Reprinted with the permission of the New Standards™.

Book Coordinator: Maria Drees

NCTE Stock Number: 46988-3050

Library of Congress Cataloging-in-Publication Data
Myers, Miles.
    Exemplar series / Miles Myers and Elizabeth Spalding.
      p.   cm.
    ISBN 0–8141–4698–8 (v. 1 : pbk.). –ISBN 0–8141–4700–3 (v. 2 : pbk.). – ISBN 0–8141–4701–1 (v. 3 : pbk.).
    1. Language arts–Ability testing–United States. 2. English language–Ability testing–United States. 3. Portfolios in education–United States. 4. Language arts–Standards–United States. I. Spalding, Elizabeth, 1951– . II. Title.
LB1576.M943 1997
  428'.0076–dc21
                                      96-47771
                                       CIP

Contents

Foreword

Are you looking for some way to show your students your goals and standards? This book will help you do that and more. The contents of this book grew out of the work of thousands of classroom teachers across the country who worked together to select and to design on-demand tasks and portfolios to assess, among other things, the contents of the *Standards for the English Language Arts* (SELA), which were developed by the National Council of Teachers of English and the International Reading Association.

The first key point to be made here is that this publication has been a large-group effort. Except for the introduction and some editing work on task descriptions, rubrics, and commentaries, the editors have been largely traffic engineers who kept one eye on the materials and another eye on the details of the NCTE/IRA standards. The on-demand tasks and portfolio entries selected for this publication were originally developed by teachers working in various state projects (e.g., California, Kentucky), in various national assessment projects (National Assessment of Educational Progress), and in various curriculum projects sponsored by NCTE. Teachers who have worked in these projects will probably find that their original work has been modified or added to during the review and piloting process.

The second key point is that the on-demand tasks and portfolios in this publication were selected because they clearly illustrated in some way how the NCTE/IRA standards for the English language arts appear in classroom assignments and student performance. The tasks were also often selected because they focused on frequently assigned literary selections and frequently assigned writing topics. Some of these tasks and portfolio entries have been "standard" for two dozen years, and some have become "standard" in recent years. The on-demand tasks and portfolio entries were also selected because the student performance, although not the very best or the very worst, was representative of the range of student performance.

The third key point is that the selections presented here are a limited sample of what is needed to assess the content of English language arts. The assessment of the standards for the English language arts requires a wide range of information—on-demand tasks, portfolio entries, multiple-choice tests, and teacher judgments of discussions and oral presentations. Multiple-choice tests and teacher judgments of discussions and oral presentations are not presented in this publication. This publication displays responses at different levels to on-demand tasks (the exemplars in the first section) and portfolio entries (the exemplars in the second section). On-demand tasks are assignments used across many classrooms, almost always with time limitations, and the portfolios are a combination of assigned and freely chosen projects, timed and untimed. On-demand tasks focus on particular standards and allow us to make comparisons across classes and districts. Portfolio entries usually tell us something unique about how each student achieves the English standards, providing evidence of how a student develops an idea over time, how several performances interact, how the student reflects about his or her work, and what the student emphasizes when allowed to make choices. We hope the exemplars—the on-demand tasks and the portfolios—will illuminate further the processes involved in achieving the NCTE/IRA standards and contribute to the ongoing conversations these standards have initiated. We want to thank all of the teachers who contributed to this project through their work on assessments across the country. We also want to thank: Maria Drees, book coordinator; Jeannette Kent, manuscript and production editor; Mimi Lee and Brent Cornwell, typesetters; and Jia Ling Yau, a graduate student, for their hard work bringing many different pieces together.

Introduction

The NCTE/IRA standards for the English language arts have three interrelated parts (see back cover): (1) the content standards themselves (NCTE/IRA, 1996); (2) descriptions of classroom practice in the *Standards Consensus* and the *Standards in Practice* series; and (3) performance standards, or the *Standards Exemplar Series*. This book is one of the three books in the *Standards Exemplar Series* and is intended for those who have wondered how teachers have translated NCTE's English language arts standards into student performance and how teachers have ranked that performance. This book will provide examples of both rankings of student work and translations of the English standards into student performances. All three books in the *Standards Exemplar Series* attempt to work within one framework with four domains of knowledge.

Two approaches are now used in the United States to describe content standards and performance standards—specification and principles/exemplification. In specification, content standards and levels of performance are usually described by small bits of behavior from one part of the language system, each specification sequenced by grade level. The answers are right or wrong, and the sequence is certain. For example, one state has mandated in its content standards that "modifiers" be taught in the elementary grades, that pronoun case be taught in middle school, and that pronoun reference be taught in high school. Clearly, however, "modifiers" and the other parts of the language system are learned throughout the grades, not just in one. Another state wants the use of commas-in-a-series taught in one grade, and commas-for-nonrestrictive-clauses or phrases taught in another. These sequences never work in the classroom. Why? Many reasons. For one thing, one part of the language system influences others. For example, the use of particular phrase and clause modifiers produces new problems in punctuation.

Although specification will not work to produce a complete list of performance standards, specification will work to identify parts of the performance standards assessing skills and content. Some knowledge in English language arts requires the specification of the names of things, and this kind of knowledge can be assessed with multiple-choice tests, which are good measures of most small-bit specifications. Sometimes a multiple choice test can assess several skills at once. For instance, a multiple choice question about reading might measure skills in decoding, comprehension, and analysis. Most national and state programs use these multiple-choice tests and describe the performance levels at each grade level as a given number of right answers. These measures are useful for some purposes, but they have serious limits. We need more emphasis on exemplification in our descriptions of performance levels.

The approach used here to describe student performance levels is exemplification. Exemplification is used by the School Curriculum and Assessment Authority of Wales and England, by the National Assessment of Educational Progress (NAEP), by the College Board, and by some states, particularly California, Kentucky, and Vermont. Exemplification is not the same as specification, or the one-part-at-a-time/one-error-at-a-time approach. In specification, counting student "errors" produces judgments of quality, but counting errors alone is not an adequate measurement of quality in exemplification. In exemplification, instead of learning one part at a time, students learn one situation at a time in reading, writing, speaking, listening, or viewing. Instead of measuring student achievement by adding up the number of right or wrong answers on a multiple-choice test, exemplification uses on-demand tasks and a range of portfolio entries to establish levels of student achievement. Exemplification then measures, with teacher judgments, the quality of performance in various situations. Exemplars show student performance on on-demand tasks in particular language situations, and exemplars in portfolios show student performance on a range of tasks over time. All portfolio entries and tasks provide evidence of growth in achieving the content standards.

The On-Demand Tasks

Performance on each on-demand task is illustrated by an *exemplar* which is accompanied by a *rubric* describing features, a *commentary* describing connections between rubrics and exemplars, and a standards index showing how each task is connected to the content standards. An *exemplar* is a sample of a student performance on a task in a given situation. Thus, in this book, levels of performance are described with (1) a description of an on-demand task, which represents one or more of the principles in the content standards and which has been tried out in many classrooms; (2) grade-level *exemplars* of student work on specific on-demand tasks requiring particular kinds of knowledge in English language arts (e.g., writing reports, responding to literature); (3) *rubrics* describing the different achievement levels for a given task and situation; and (4) *commentaries* showing the relationship of each sample to the rubric. In grades 4–5, three achievement levels—high, middle, and low—are presented for each on-demand task. In K–3, three development levels—emergent, early, and fluent—are used. The achievement levels and portraits of development make visible the values and standards that teachers share. On-demand tasks sometimes are used only for assessment. Sometimes they are used only for classroom instruction; sometimes for both.

The Portfolio Tasks

A portfolio is a collection, taken over time, of student performances on classroom assignments. These assignments are tasks showing the student's performance in a range of knowledge domains in English language arts, the student's development throughout the year, and the processes used by students in various tasks—all based on the content standards. This book presents three portfolios which exemplify achievement on the standards in grades 4–5. Each has been ranked at one of three achievement levels: high, middle, or low. For each entry in the portfolio, marginal comments based on a rubric will highlight strengths and weaknesses of that particular piece. Following each portfolio is a summary commentary which links the portfolio as a whole to the rubrics and marginal comments.

The Rubrics

The rubrics that accompany the student samples in this book are drawn from several rubrics and frameworks for assessing student performances in English language arts. The only requirement was that these rubrics and frameworks be consistent with the NCTE/IRA content standards. Rubrics usually focus on particular kinds of writing or particular purposes and audiences, giving general descriptors of several levels of performance. In the *Exemplar Series,* the introduction describes the content standards as kinds of knowledge and activities, and the rubrics are situation-specific and achievement-level-specific.

The Commentaries

In exemplification, a description of an achievement level must have three parts: samples or exemplars of performance, rubric, and commentary. All three are necessary. The commentary describes the links between rubrics and samples, pointing to specific evidence from the sample and adding evaluations of the overall work.

Connections to Standards

On-demand tasks and items in the portfolios are indexed to one or more of the NCTE/IRA standards. For each task, target standards are those directly met by the assignment. Supplementary standards are those which are met when the task is embedded in a larger instructional unit. Instruction always involves many standards at any one time.

STANDARDS IN THE CLASSROOM

Standards for the English Language Arts (SELA) tells us that in the classroom we will find (1) students who are playing the roles of readers and writers, discovering how to shape their experience and to connect their experience to text; (2) evidence of public audiences, classroom audiences, and personal audiences playing the roles of reader and responder to student work; (3) subject matter, whether imaginary, public/civic, or academic and informational; (4) different tools (computers, telephones, calculators, faxes) and editing groups; (5) various texts both literary and nonliterary for reading, hearing, and viewing; (6) reference books on the structure of English (phonology, morphology, syntax) and text; and (7) evidence of cognitive and metacognitive development in drafts from editing, discussion, and response groups, including learning logs, outlines, notes, and other forms.

From the student work in a typical classroom, teachers have specified some kinds of performance as particularly salient: (1) narrative writing (fiction or autobiography and biography), (2) report writing (newspaper reports, portraits, information summaries), (3) argument writing (editorials, letters of complaint, persuasive essay), (4) reading depth—response to literature (character evaluation, story comparisons, and evaluations, summaries), (5) reading depth—response to informational texts (history, general information, bus schedules), (6) reading breadth (reading journals, book logs), (6) visual representation, including mapping and charts, (8) skill development (skill logs, showing print or spelling changes), and (9) imaginative tasks (drawings, poems). These are not the only performances of importance, but they are common performances in English language arts and are stressed in *Standards for the English Language Arts*. Each of the three books in this exemplar series (K–5, 6–8, 9–12) includes most of these types, but not necessarily all. Evidence of speaking, listening, and viewing rarely appear in the three books.

A FRAMEWORK FOR ASSESSMENT

What do exemplars of on-demand tasks and portfolios tell us about what students know and are able to do? Exemplars of on-demand tasks and portfolios exhibit the standards in action in *three ways of knowing,* in *six activities or forms of representation,* in *four domains of knowledge* in English language arts, and in *various patterns of student development.*

Three Ways of Knowing

The three ways of knowing are, first, declarative or content knowledge ("knowing that"), including the knowledge usually exhibited by students in traditional multiple-choice tests ("The main character is a spider"); second, procedural or process knowledge ("knowing how"), including the use of reading strategies, writing strategies, and strategies for turning various kinds of knowledge into action; and third, background or general awareness knowledge, including a general awareness of how to use language for different purposes ("knowing about/why").

I. *Knowing that* is the factual, informational knowledge of English language arts, including information about genre, literary forms, and rules of spelling or punctuation or subject-verb agreement (see the four domains of knowledge below). *Knowing that* is developed through use, memorization, and multiple readings. It can often be assessed with multiple-choice tests, but this approach alone is inadequate. Constructed responses reveal how well the students know information in context.

II. *Knowing how* is the procedural or process knowledge of external action, of using the four domains of knowledge in an actual situation. One can name the parts of a sentence (*knowing that*) and still not be able to write one (*knowing how*). *Knowing how* requires assessment during the use of language and is best evaluated in a performance assessment. Six uses are emphasized here: reading, writing, speaking, listening, viewing, and representing (see activities below). The uses are usually embedded in particular events in the classroom.

III. *Knowing about* is a general awareness of language structure and use. It requires a broad awareness of contexts for language use and experiences with many situations requiring variations in language use. *Knowing about* requires the use of metaphors and analogies to capture the overall sense of something and is developed through broad exploration and choice. Assessments of Breadth of Reading is an example of assessment focusing on *knowing about*. *Knowing about* can be assessed in both multiple-choice tests and constructed responses.

These three ways of knowing—knowing that, knowing how, and knowing about—shape the breadth and depth of knowledge from the four domains of English language arts—cognition, rhetoric, linguistics/conventions, and cultural themes or ideas from the humanities (see Figure 1, p. xviii). These three ways of knowing and four domains of knowledge interact in the six activities of English language arts.

Six Activities or Forms of Representation

The six activities or forms of representation of English language arts are reading, writing, speaking, listening, viewing, and representing. Students who prepare graphics for a speech or a filmed drama are engaged in representing in English. Viewing refers to the knowledge needed to comprehend a graphic (e.g., a bus schedule), an illustration, or a filmed drama.

Four Domains of Knowledge

I. *Cognition* involves three kinds of internal cognitive processes. Two are strategies:

- strategies for fluent processing in basic <u>decoding</u> (refers to learning the code in reading) and <u>encoding</u> (refers to learning the code in writing);

- strategies for <u>metacognitive processing</u> (thinking about thinking), including processes for initial understanding, putting ideas together (interpretation), connecting personal experience and text, summarizing and paraphrasing, and developing a critical stance;

- the third cognitive process involves <u>self-awareness and habits-of-mind</u>: a tolerance of ambiguity, tolerance of the need to review and reread, of uncertainty, tolerance of the need to take risks in one's estimates and guesses, and an awareness of one's "life story."

II. *Rhetoric* refers to interactions among narrator, audience, subject, and types of discourse (literary, information):

- <u>distance to an audience</u> (Is the audience close or distant?): students learn such things as how to shift in their writing from close, conversational audiences to the distant, formal audiences of public discourse;

- <u>distance to a subject</u> (Is the subject personal or impersonal?): students learn such things as how to distinguish between narrators who are in the past or present, here or there, participants or observers, and narrators who are providing information or interpretations;

- <u>narrator perspective</u>: students learn different perspectives—telling and showing, reliable and unreliable narrators, serious and comic, indirect (ironical) and direct, formal and informal;

- <u>reader stance</u>: students learn to shift from the poetic (literary) to the transanctional (information) stance in their reading and writing, and in their viewing and representing.

III. *Linguistics/Conventions* refers to three kinds of language structures and practices:

- alphabet structure: students develop a sense of what letters are (relationships to sound), how to make them (write), and how they blend together or are segmented when they are used to represent the units of oral language;

- text structures: paragraphs, meter, rhyme, figures of speech, literary forms, and so forth. For example, students learn things about the structure of narratives, descriptions, or arguments;

- language structure (grammar): students learn about phonology (sound), morphology (words), and syntax (phrases and sentences). In the early elementary years, students develop phonemic awareness and a word sense. Phonemes, which are sounds, make a difference. The motor skills for writing, sentence awareness, and a sense of text as a message are also part of elementary growth.

- conventions (mechanics): students learn about spelling, punctuation, usage, capitalization, and other editing forms. Each school site needs a style or convention guide to help teachers and students focus on conventions of special significance. It is clear that students learn to read and to write by reading and writing; sometimes, however, students need to isolate parts of language for focused observation. Students are often tested on some combination of these kinds of knowledge about language.

What are some ways of dividing up the parts of language? The National Assessment of Educational Progress used the following analysis of language structure and conventions to analyze student writing (Applebee, Langer, and Mullis, 1987):

A. Sentence Types

1. Simple: A sentence that contains a subject and a verb. It may also have an object, subject complement, phrase, nominative absolute, or verbal. Also a word group used in dialogue, for emphasis, or as an exclamation that is not an independent clause.

2. Compound: A sentence containing two or more simple sentences joined by something other than a comma.

3. Complex (and compound-complex): A sentence that contains at least one independent clause and one dependent clause.

4. Run-on

a. Fused: A sentence containing two or more independent clauses with no punctuation or conjunction separating them.

b. On and on: A sentence consisting of four or more independent clauses strung together with conjunctions.

c. Comma splice: A sentence containing two or more independent clauses separated by a comma instead of a semicolon or a coordinating conjunction.

5. Fragment: A word group, other than an independent clause, written and punctuated as a sentence.

B. Faulty Sentence Construction

1. Agreement Error: A sentence in which at least one of the following occurs: subject and verb do not agree, pronoun and antecedent do not agree, noun and modifier do not agree, subject/object pronoun is misused, or verb tense shifts.

2. Awkward Sentence

    a. Faulty parallelism: A parallel construction that is semantically or structurally dysfunctional.

    b. Unclear pronoun reference: A pronoun's antecedent is unclear.

    c. Illogical construction: Faulty modification or a dangling modifier, or a functionally misarranged or misproportioned sentence.

    d. Other dysfunctions: A sentence containing an omitted or extra word, or a split construction that definitely detracts from readability.

C. Punctuation Errors

Errors of commission and errors of omission in the use of commas, dashes, quotation marks, semicolons, apostrophes, and end marks.

D. Problems in Word-Level Conventions

1. Word Choice: The writer needs a word that is different from the one written. This category also includes attempts at a verb, adjective, or adverb form that is nonexistent or unacceptable.

2. Spelling: In addition to a misspelling, this category includes word-division errors at the end of a line, two words written as one, one word written as two, superfluous plurals, and groups of distinguishable letters that do not make a legitimate word.

3. Capitalization: The first word in a sentence is not capitalized, a proper noun or adjective within a sentence is not capitalized, or the pronoun "I" is not capitalized.

IV. *Cultural Themes or Ideas* include three kinds of concepts from the humanities:

- <u>core concepts</u> like the ideas of the past and future, the hero, friendship, coming of age, setting, character, and ethics, among others. These core concepts are part of the central narratives of English language arts;

- <u>dual concepts</u> like stance (poetic and transactional), multiculturalism or pluralism (difference and commonality), choice (freedom and fate), foreshadowing (ambiguity and predictability), community (individual and society), and organization (rational and intuitive), among others;

- <u>metaphorical concepts</u> that structure the narratives of English language arts (e.g., the world as a machine with part-whole relationships, life as an organism with growth over time, knowledge as a mirror or lamp, democracy as a search for common bonds). Metaphors and analogies are critical in *knowing about*.

A word needs to be said about the materials or texts focusing on the fourth domain, the ideas of English language arts. Remember that cognition, rhetoric (different audiences), and linguistics/conventions (text and conventions) are the other three domains of knowledge in English language arts, and we have grammar books, composition texts, and strategy lists to help us think about those three domains. But what books and materials help us think about the fourth domain, the ideas of English language arts? English language arts teachers across the country attempt to answer this question when they select literature for a given grade level. In literature, students learn ideas in context (honesty, heroism, truth, cowardice, deceit, ambiguity, culture, gender, age, modernism, romanticism, and magic).

The following are a few of the texts typically used in the elementary years. Consult the Standards in Practice and Standards Consensus series, both published by NCTE, for other examples.

Poetry

Oxford Book of Poetry for Children (Blishen and Wildsmith), *The Random House Book of Mother Goose* (Lobel, ed.), *Red Dog, Blue Fly: Poems for a Football Season* (Mathis), *Where the Sidewalk Ends* (Silverstein)

Picture/Fantasy and Realism, K–2

Corduroy (Freeman), *Bread and Jam for Frances* (Hoban), *Harold and the Purple Crayon* (Johnson), *The Little Engine That Could* (Piper), *The Tale of Peter Rabbit* (Potter), *Where the Wild Things Are* (Sendak), *Harry the Dirty Dog* (Zion), *There's a Nightmare in My Closet* (Mayer)*, Alexander and the Terrible, Horrible, No Good, Very Bad Day* (Viorst), *Petunia* (DuVoisin), *Sam* (Scott), *Is Your Mama a Llama?* (Guarino), *Sylvester and the Magic Pebble* (Steig), *Danny and the Dinosaur* (Hoff), *The Very Hungry Caterpillar* (Carle), *Curious George* (Rey), *Amelia Bedelia* (Parish), *Ira Sleeps Over* (Waber), *Mike Mulligan and His Steam Shovel* (Burton), *One Fine Day* (Hogrogian), and *Tikki Tikki Tembo* (Mosel)

Realistic Fiction, Fantasy, Informational, Grades 3–5

The Emperor's New Clothes (Andersen), *A Bear Called Paddington* (Bond), *Ramona and Her Father* (Cleary), *The 500 Hats of Bartholomew Cubbins* (Seuss), *Sam, Bangs, and Moonshine* (Ness), *The Fables of Aesop* (Aesop [Jacobs]), *The Wonderful Flight to the Mushroom Planet* (Cameron), *James and the Giant Peach* (Dahl), *The Wind in the Willows* (Grahame), *Frederick Douglass: The Black Lion* (McKissack), *The Mysteries of Harris Burdick* (Van Allsburg), *Charlotte's Web* (White), *The Gift Giver* (Hansen), *Ben and Me* (Lawson), *Child of the Owl* (Yep), *Sarah, Plain and Tall* (MacLachlan), *And Then What Happened, Paul Revere?* (Fritz), *Koko's Kitten* (Patterson), *The Little House on the Prairie* (Wilder), *Caddie Woodlawn* (Brink), *Magic School Bus* (Cole), *If You Made a Million* (Schwartz), *Millions of Cats* (Gag), *The Patchwork Quilt* (Flournoy), *Pippi Longstocking* (Lindgren), *Hatchet* (Paulsen), *Runaway Ralph* (Cleary), *Tales of a 4th Grade Nothing* (Blume), *Superfudge* (Blume), and *I Sailed with Columbus* (Schlein)

These lists and others like them are intended to help teachers at the local level generate their own discussion about what books might be selected. The central point is that students read and describe narratives about our common humanity, our border crossings across time and space, our building of a democratic community. Within these narratives, we find a body of core concepts, informing metaphors, and dualisms.

Patterns of Development

In this book, the K–3 samples, from students up to age nine or ten, are presented as portraits of development. Up to about age ten, students are developing many distinctions among the functions of language, various sign systems, uses of tools, different understandings of the self, and so forth. Children bring to their experiences a basic mental architecture which is elaborated through interactions with the world. Early on, the child works with *procedural representations* (looking, clutching, turning head, twisting body). The developmental sequence up to age ten might be characterized, according to Katherine Nelson (1996), as four different kinds of representation, each with its own set of interactions and understanding. In *episodic representation,* the child explores images, space, movement, sound, taste, sensor-motor procedures (reaching, holding, turning the head) within situated models of events—lunch, bedtime, playpen time, and so forth. The child's brain at birth has the basic architecture for at least two memory systems, one for general procedures (reaching), and another for specific episodes (lunch). The episode, says Nelson, is the basic building block of cognitive development (Nelson, 1996: 84).

Later, according to Nelson (1996), the child begins to imitate and simulate models of events (playing lunch, giving the doll a bath) which they have experienced. In this period of *mimetic representation* the child begins to learn games requiring imitation and reciprocal relations (peekaboo, patty-cake). Later the child projects familiar routines onto metaphorical props (the broom becomes a horse, the block becomes a car), and even assembles tools for simulated events. These mimetic activities develop the child's capacity to represent or re-present various episodes. As models of events are added to the child's repertoire of imitations, children continue to differentiate self from others (role playing), to distinguish one function of language from another, and to distinguish pretend (imaginative) from actual (transactional).

Around age three or four children are exploring *narrative or mythic representation.* The culture here is very much like a typical preschool or kindergarten in which children tell riddles and stories and make up events which are not scripts or events they have experienced. In *narrative representation,* the child both draws pictures, writes marks on paper, tells and reads stories (or pretends to read), building distinctions among sign systems (gestures, drawings, oral stories, numbers) and genres (autobiography and biography). As children reach for new words and ideas to add to stories, core concepts like *dog* are differentiated into specific types such as *collie* and *bulldog.*

The work of the K–5 students reflects efforts to capture *procedures* (holding the pencil), *episodes* (the trip), *imitations* (what Dad did), *narration* (story), and *theory* (why). Throughout these years, the child is developing the necessary distinctions among sounds, letters, words, sentences, drawing and print, episodes and stories. The child is literally growing a brain with the necessary phonological, morphological, and syntactic connections to make reading and writing a fluent process. Around age nine or ten (fourth grade), the child begins to explore in more detail what Nelson calls the *representations of external theory and external memory storage* (the library) which are typical of the subjects of schooling.

In this book, the four domains of knowledge (cognition, rhetoric, linguistics/ conventions, themes/ideas) are represented in the rubrics and commentaries as different kinds of developmental tensions among and between different ways of knowing. For example:

I. Cognition:

A. Sensori-motor and Perceptual Knowing   vs.   Symbolic Knowing

Example: The child first may know something by seeing or touching, and later the child knows things by reading.

B. Slow Decoding/Encoding   vs.   Fluent Processing
Fragmented Knowing   *Automatic Knowing*

Example: In development, the writer's slow marks can, with interaction and help, slowly develop into fluent alphabetic writing.

C. Mentoring   vs.   Metacognition: Thinking about Thinking
Extensive scaffolding (help) by others   *Selected scaffolding (help) by others;*
Fragmented tool use   *internal self-scaffolding, control of*
                                      tools, and capacity to analyze or
                                      integrate fluent processing above

Example: In development, the writer or reader may begin with extensive assistance and move to more fully internalized habits of reflection or thinking.

D. Memory   vs.   Reason and Reflection
Learning by procedural or   *Learning also by semantic memory*
episodic memory only   *and reason/reflection*

Example: In development, the writer or reader may begin with associations and habits, later copying and memorizing, and still later, analyzing, critiquing, and revising.

II. Rhetoric:

A. Scaffolds of Limited Interactions   vs.   Frames for Extended Interactions
Close/personal   *Far/impersonal*

B. Audience   vs.   External Communities as Audience
Close/personal   *Far/impersonal*

(continued on next page)

C. Subject   vs.   External World as Subject
Close/personal, expressive   *Detached ("objective")*

Example: In development, the writer often begins with close, personal audiences and subjects and moves toward more flexibility, including distant audiences and subjects. At the same time, the student is showing growth in social interactions with others. In the elementary years, the social development of children is a foundation for their rhetorical skills.

D. Direct, Imitative Perspective   vs.   Indirect Perspective
                                           Irony/comedy

Example: In development, the writer or reader appears to begin with a mimetic or direct perspective and later adds the indirect perspectives of comedy, irony, and others.

E. Simple Pretend   vs.   Real Events
Elaborated Poetic   *Transactional*
(Imaginative literature)   *(Informational texts)*

Example: The child begins with pretend vs. real events and later develops an elaborated understanding of literary and nonliterary materials.

III. Linguistics/Conventions:

A. Language/Text—Small Forms   vs.   Language/Text—Larger Forms
                                           Synthetic/narrative structures and
                                           Analytic Features/Paradigmatic Structures

Example: In development, the student often begins with gestures, sounds, and words and later moves toward some use of narrative and analytical forms.

B. Oral Forms Only   vs.   Oral and Written Forms

Example: In development, the writer or reader often begins with knowledge about small oral forms (sound-letter correspondence, phonemic sense, word meanings, sentence sense) and later adds an elaborated understanding of sentences, paragraphs, and stories in both oral and written forms.

IV. Themes or Ideas:

A. Ideas/Themes   vs.   Scientific/Academic
Folk/everyday   *Concepts and Definitions*
Ideas/concepts
(Place, time, directions)

Example: In development, the writer often moves from everyday forms of knowledge such as prototype knowledge of dog to an understanding of academic forms of knowledge such as superordinate categories like animal and mineral.

These are not the only developmental patterns which teachers have identified in the work of students at different ages. But these patterns illustrate some of the variations teachers attend to when they are trying to estimate growth in the English language arts. In writing and responding to literature, for example, the student is often experiencing the tensions between the personal response, which connects the text to one's internal experiences or one's values, and the analytical response, which connects the text to other texts and to ideas from the external world. The student may also be experiencing the tension between a case (for example, an autobiography) and a more generalized exposition (a larger intertextual pattern involving several cases). The student may also be trying to tell the narrative of boundary crossings, experiencing the tensions between tradition or the new and the past or present. In each instance, these tensions are part of a developmental pattern which influences the student's performance. Some of the other tensions of developmental patterns are suggested in Figure 2 on p. xix.

CONNECTIONS TO STANDARDS

The four domains of knowledge in English language arts are described in many places in *Standards for the English Language Arts.* For example:

    1. *Cognition* is described in Standards 3, 5, and 10. For example: "If [students] are reading something that is especially challenging or foreign to them, they

may need to pause frequently to search for graphic, phonological, syntactic, and semantic clues that will help them make sense of the text" (page 32).

2. *Rhetoric* is described in Standards 4, 7, and 12. For example: "Even handwriting can reflect a consideration of audience: scribbles may work when writing personal notes; however, directions to others on how to get to an unknown destination will most likely require clear and complete writing" (page 34).

3. *Linguistics/conventions* are described in Standards 6, 9, and 11. For example: "Students need a working knowledge of the systems and structures of language as well as familiarity with accepted language conventions, including grammar, punctuation, spelling, and the formal elements of visual texts" (page 36).

4. *Themes or ideas* are described in Standards 1, 2, and 8. For example: Literary works "give students opportunities to engage in ethical and philosophical reflection on the values and beliefs of their own cultures, of other cultures, and of other times and places" (page 30).

The six activities or forms of representation are also described in the standards:

1. *Reading:* Standards 1, 2, and 3 describe the content and processes of reading.

2. *Writing:* Standards 4, 5, and 6 describe the content and processes of writing.

3. *Speaking:* Standards 4 and 12 describe the emphasis on speaking.

4. *Listening:* Standards 7, 8, and 9 emphasize the importance of listening.

5. *Viewing:* Standard 3 introduces the importance of comprehending and interpreting visuals, and high school vignette 5 gives an example of the importance of film study.

6. *Representing:* Standard 4 introduces the use of visual language, and middle school vignette 2 provides an example of mapping.

The standards also call for all three ways of knowing: knowing that, knowing how, and knowing about. To match standards and assessments, teachers are urged to review *Standards for the English Language Arts* carefully.

Each section of this book contains descriptions of how various on-demand tasks and portfolio entries represent achievement of the English standards. Because this book presents samples of students responding to challenges representing one or more of the standards for the English language arts, you can use this book to illustrate what the NCTE English standards might look like in practice. Many parts of the standards for the English language arts are not represented here. For example, discussion, dramatic activities, and performance on multiple-choice tests are not included. In addition, no attempt has been made to include the *full* range of student responses. Nevertheless, the samples contained in this book should help you paint a portrait of some of your goals in the English language arts.

In the design of the book, we have made it easy to see how the on-demand tasks and portfolios illustrate the NCTE/IRA English standards. Open up the first flap of the back cover and notice that the standards are on your right, and the samples are on your left. Of course, the list of standards included here is not a substitute for their full explanation and discussion in *Standards for the English Language Arts,* to which we refer you, but it can help you in mapping standards to exemplars. Teachers at NCTE's 1996 Spring Conference in Boston, for example, tried mapping NCTE/IRA standards to particular student performances, and those teachers found, as you will find, that the exemplars often incorporate many standards. In addition, you can use the other two books in the *Standards Exemplar Series* (for grades 6–8 and 9–12) to see how the exemplars for particular standards change across the grades. By looking through all three exemplar books, you will find that in general students at particular ages do better on some tasks.

Figure 1 shows another way of thinking about the three types of knowledge. That is, taken together, *knowing that, knowing how, and knowing about* may be viewed as constituting breadth and depth in reading, writing, speaking, listening, viewing, and representing.

Figure 1: Sample Performances for Assessing Breadth and Depth in the English Language Arts

The Three Types of Knowledge in the Six Activities	The Four Domains of Knowledge in the English Language Arts			
	Cognition: Processing	Rhetoric: Distancing	Linguistics/Conventions: Grammar Structures, Text Structures, and Conventions	Themes/Ideas: Constructing
Reading: Breadth and Depth (*knowing that, knowing how, and knowing about*)	Shows fluency in reading Makes correct guesses about thoughts of characters	Depth: Reads in depth—first-person narrator Breadth: Reads a range of narrators	Reads a range of forms—poems, novels, short stories, magazines, newspapers	Traces a single idea in history Reads a range of opinions by different authors on same issue
Writing: Breadth and Depth (*knowing that, knowing how, and knowing about*)	Shows automaticity in handwriting Shows evidence of editing conventions Drafts of argument show strategies of questioning, believing, disbelieving, summarizing, clarifying	Shows ability to shift point of view of work—from first to second person Writes to three different audiences on public issue	Shows ability to write in different literary forms—poems, short stories—and in different nonliterary forms—reports, editorials, letters, features	Shows sense of theme, place, and character in writing of literary text
Breadth and Depth in *Speaking and Listening* (*knowing that, knowing how, and knowing about*)	Shows fluency in speaking Drafts show use of multiple sources in development of speech	Leads small-group discussion and then reports or listens to large-group in large-group discussion	Uses diverse structures in speech, from narrative to exposition and argument	Gives speech to class on public issue
Viewing: Breadth and Depth (*knowing that, knowing how, and knowing about*)	Shows fluency in reading graphs Makes correct location of bus times	Can redo line graph as bar graph	Understands flashback device in film	Can summarize plot of film
Representing: Breadth and Depth (*knowing that, knowing how, and knowing about*)	Can organize portfolio in some kind of sequence		Can produce a clear table of contents	Can organize book log by theme

These three kinds of knowledge from four different domains develop in different ways throughout the grades. Therefore, the performance of students will show some typical developmental patterns which are reflected in the samples, rubrics, and commentaries. These developmental patterns are presented in Figure 2.

Figure 2: Typical Patterns of Development in Domains of English Language Arts

	The Four Domains of Knowledge in the English Language Arts							
	Cognition: Processing		Rhetoric: Distancing		Linguistics/Conventions: Grammar Structures, Text Structures, and Conventions		Themes/Ideas: Constructing	
	Encoding/ Decoding	Processing and Metacognitive Strategies	Distance from Audience	Distance from Subject	Text Structure	Grammar Modeling	Core Concepts	Dual Concepts
Some Typical **Developmental** **Patterns**	From experience to mapping/ drawing to print code From garbles and fragments to conventions and fluency From need for much assistance to selected scaffolding	From recording to reporting to generalizing From processing procedures to thinking about thinking	From expressive audience (self) to distant public audiences	From first-person experience to third-person reflections	Text: from narrative to paradigmatic modes Conventions: from letter (print) to sounds; from word (spelling) to phrase (commas)	Grammar: from sound to word to phrase Grammar: from additive to embedded structures	From the sense of an idea to the structure of an idea From everyday concepts like "the hero" to scientific/academic concepts like "the psychology of leadership"	

If you open out the standards page, you will see a framework for assessing student performance in the English language arts. This framework is explained in detail on pages x–xvi of this introduction. As you study and discuss the exemplars and portfolios, you can use the framework to generate your own descriptive statements about what a particular piece of student work shows about what a student knows and can do. The framework on the inside back flap contains some sample "starter" statements. On the innermost side of the back cover is a chart cross-referencing the on-demand tasks and the portfolio pieces. You can use this chart to locate additional examples of particular kinds of performances (e.g., reports of information) and to identify differences and similarities between on-demand tasks and portfolio pieces. The list of various kinds of performances in on-demand tasks and portfolios appears in the table of contents.

Finally, you should use this book to start discussions with students, with fellow teachers, and with parents about achievement levels in the range and the depth of understanding English and the English language arts. In portfolios showing several items from one student, you will find that a poor performance on one or two tasks does not necessarily represent what a student potentially can do, and by looking at a collection of tasks from one student, you will find out something about the student's range of skills in the English language arts. We urge you to share the student samples with your students and to ask your students to rank the samples, to write comments explaining their rankings, and then to share this information with other students. We recommend that teachers order a class set of the series in order to illustrate for students what portfolios look like and what various assignments look like. We also suggest that you ask parents to rank samples and discuss their rankings together. We recommend that you do the same with fellow teachers. Try scoring the student samples yourself, alone or with others, and then compare your rankings with those in the book. The rankings, the commentaries, and the rubrics come from many places across the country and have been tried out in many places, but that does not mean that your local ranking might not involve an insight into a work which the others missed. We will reserve space on NCTE's Web site for an electronic discussion of your responses (http://www.ncte.org).

REFERENCES

Applebee, A. N., Langer, J., & Mullis, I. V. S. (1987). *Grammar, punctuation, and spelling: Controlling the conventions of written English at ages 9, 13, and 17.* NAEP Report No. 15–W03. Princeton, NJ: Educational Testing Service.

Nelson, K. (1996). *Language in Cognitive Development: The Emergence of the Mediated Mind.* Melbourne, Australia: Cambridge University Press.

Exemplars

This section contains exemplars of performances commonly expected of students in grades K–5. Each exemplar consists of a description of a task, a sample of student performance, a rubric describing the developmental or achievement level of that performance, and a commentary showing the relationship of the performance to the rubric. Exemplars from students in grades K–3 are characterized as "emergent," "early," or "fluent," in order to show various stages of literacy development. Exemplars from students in grades 4–5 are ranked as "high," "middle," or "low."

At the end of each set of exemplars is a graphic ("Connections to Standards") showing which standards for the English language arts are targeted in a particular performance. The second line of the graphic suggests additional standards that might be illustrated if the task were extended or embedded in a larger unit of classroom instruction. You can easily reference the standards by folding out the back flap of this book.

The K–3 exemplars in this section were selected from a variety of sources, including published samples of student work and work collected by classroom teachers who assisted in this project. The grades 4 and 5 exemplars were selected from similar sources, as well as state (e.g., California) and national (e.g., National Assessment of Educational Progress, the New Standards Project) assessments.

Some of the exemplars have been slightly altered from their original format. In some cases, original scoring rubrics have been revised to reflect the framework presented in the introduction of this book and on its inside back cover. Also, numerical scores which may have been originally assigned do not appear in this book. For example, student work from California's assessment of reading and writing was scored by California teachers on a scale of 0–6. In this book, student work from grades 4 and 5 is described as being in the high, middle, or low *range* of performance. This book is not intended to be a scoring system; rather, it suggests how you might go about creating your own scoring system.

Task

In SIPM (Social Interaction, Pictures, and Marks), students are asked to use paper and the available instruments (crayons, pencils) to "Tell a story," "Write a valentine card," "Show us something about _____." The task is broadly defined in order to allow children many points of entry.

Exemplar

Rubric

Cognition: The children begin to develop sensori-motor coordination and control, enabling them to center their marks and to create margins.

Rhetoric: Children are aware that pictures and marks on paper can be messages to other people. However, for many children, the primary purpose of student "papers" is to enhance interactions with other students and the teacher. The papers are a device for sharing and talking.

Linguistics/Language: Children begin to distinguish among random marks, pictures, and "print" (or marks which look like printed letters).

Commentary

The emergent work of children, using clay, talk, crayons, pencils, felt-tip markers, "reading" aloud and other instruments, begins to differentiate among: (1) the different sections of the paper on which they are working (margins, top, bottom, center); (2) the differences among signs (stick figures, pictures, marks, letters); and (3) the different units of languages (letters, sound units or phonemes, words, sentences or phrases). These differentiations take place within social interactions, which are themselves segmented into different episodes (lunch, grocery shopping, bedtime, recess, reading time).

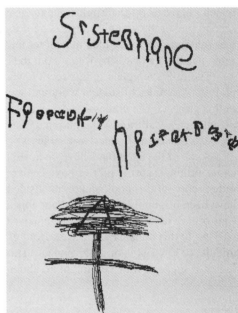

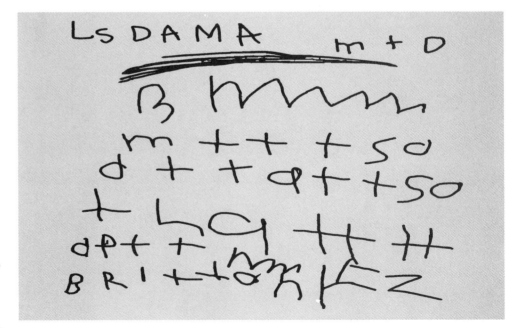

Exemplar

Commentary

Great strides toward school literacy are evident in early writing. Pictures and print, which are now clearly distinct, begin to be used together to convey a message, and different words are clearly separated from each other. The names of people, places, and things become increasingly important to the child as a device for getting some control over the world. Naming the world is an important part of being in the world.

Exemplar

Fluent

R u b r i c

Cognition: Excellent cognitive control of (1) sensori-motor routines (holding pencil) and (2) awareness of total composition.

Rhetoric: The child is attempting to maintain frontal stance toward the audience (see head of dog turned toward audience). The frontal position of things and objects is one of the first attempts of children to incorporate audience awareness into composition. Side views come later.

Linguistics: Sign distinctions are clear (drawing and language), and language distinctions (letter, word, sentence) are impressive. The space between words shows a conscious effort to segment words, a necessary step toward sentence composition. In early material, words were segmented with dark lines between them or different lines (see previous page). Here the writer uses space, a very heroic move.

Commentary

Chris Ault, a teacher from Columbus, Ohio, developed her own system for separating the children's work into different types: (1) picture, (2) numbers, (3) picture with something like letters, (4) like-letters, (5) picture w/random letters, (6) picture with known word, (7) known word, (8) copy from environment (see early samples), (9) record of random message, (10) record of invented message, and (11) record of message with known situation. A chart of these trends in Ault's class is shown below. The evolved sample above shows an effort at a sentence message, which is probably an invented message.

Qualities	1st GP		totals	2nd GP		totals	3rd GP		totals
Picture	16	32%	32	9	14%	19	4	5%	8
Numbers	0	0%	64%	6	12%	30%	3	4%	11%
Picture w/Letter-Like Symbols	1	2%		1	2%		0	0%	
Letter-Like Symbols	5	10%		1	2%		0	0%	
Picture w/Random Letters	10	20%		2	3%		1	1%	
Random Letters	9	18%	14	26	41%	36	6	8%	39
Picture w/Known Word	1	2%	28%	1	2%	57%	0	0%	49%
Known Word	0	0%		4	6%		22	29%	
Copy from Environment	4	8%		5	8%		9	12%	
Record Message Using Random Letters	2	4%	4	4	6%	8	2	3%	30
Record Message Using Invented Spelling	1	2%	8%	2	2%	13%	13	17%	40%
Record Message Using Known Words	1	2%		2	2%		15	20%	
Total Writing Samples	50			63			75		188

Connections to Standards

	STANDARDS											
Targeted	1	2	3	4	5	6	7	8	9	10	11	12
Supplementary	1	2	3	4	5	6	7	8	9	10	11	12

Beginning writers experiment with print, visual language, spatial elements, and form in order to communicate with familiar audiences for particular purposes (4). As students develop skill in writing, they acquire a broad repertoire of writing strategies (5) and a range of knowledge about language structure and conventions (6) which enable them to create print texts for a variety of purposes and audiences.

Task

Teachers in Kentucky used tasks like the following to assess phonemic awareness and knowledge of alphabet. In one case, the teacher gave the students in an ungraded primary class the following sequence of problems: (1) name 26 upper case letters (teacher shows the letters in random order, and the student names the letter); (2) give the sound of each letter above as that letter would sound in a word; (3) give a word beginning with or containing the letter; and (4) name the lower case letters (presented in random order). The teacher records student responses and then graphs the results. One can speculate about what the student knows. Problem two, for example, can be easily misinterpreted by students. Nevertheless, most students learned how to do the task.

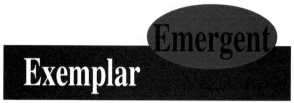

Exemplar — Emergent

Legend

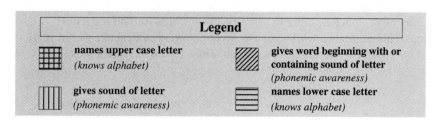

▦ **names upper case letter** *(knows alphabet)*	▨ **gives word beginning with or containing sound of letter** *(phonemic awareness)*
▥ **gives sound of letter** *(phonemic awareness)*	▤ **names lower case letter** *(knows alphabet)*

Rubric

1. Knows 21 letters as caps.

2. Knows 0 sounds of letters in isolation.

3. Knows how to use two letters in words.

4. Knows 18 letters in small caps.

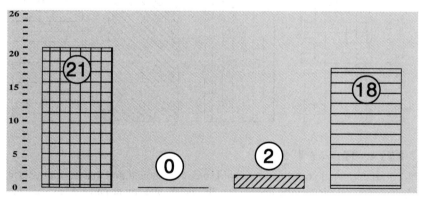

Commentary

In March of her kindergarten year, this student showed the emerging ability to connect symbols, sounds, and words. She named the majority of letters, as both upper and lower case. She did not appear to know the sounds of letters in isolation. She connected the word "pig" to the letter "p" and "snake" to the letter "s."

Exemplar — Early

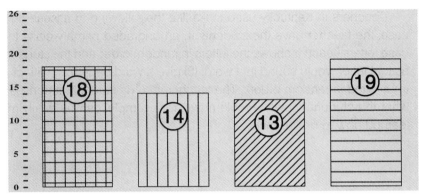

R u b r i c

1. Knows 18 letters as caps.

2. Knows 14 of the 18 letters as sounds.

3. Knows 13 of the 18 as letters in words.

4. Knows 19 letters as small caps.

Commentary

In March of his kindergarten year, this student demonstrated that he was progressing quite well. He recognized most of the letters in upper and lower case and could give the sound of slightly more than half of them. He suggested words for half the letters, although some of his examples, while creative, were not good evidence, e.g., "M & M (m), X-Files (x), T-Ball (t). He deserves congratulations for his inventive strategy.

Exemplar — Fluent

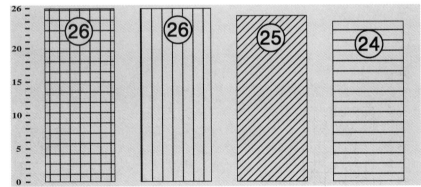

R u b r i c

1. Knows all letters as caps.

2. Knows all letters as sounds in words.

3. Knows use of letters in words.

4. Knows 24 of the 26 letters as small caps.

Commentary

In April of her kindergarten year, this 5-year-old student demonstrated mastery of the task. She made only two errors—identifying lower-case "b" as "d" and lower-case "g" as "q." She could not suggest a word containing the sound of "x." The words she suggested as examples were quite sophisticated, including "quiet" (q), "itching" (i), "oval" (o), and "Venus" (v).

Connections to Standards

	STANDARDS											
Targeted	1	2	*3*	4	5	6	7	8	9	10	11	12
Supplementary	*1*	*2*	*3*	4	5	6	7	8	9	10	11	12

This task targets awareness of the relationships between letters and sounds, and letters and words, an important skill for beginning readers (3). This inventory is but one of many ways teachers document and analyze the progress of young readers and writers. As students develop skill and fluency, they are able to read a wide range of literary and nonliterary, print and nonprint texts (1, 2).

Task

The task is a spelling test. The student is given the word, and the student writes the word in the *write* column. Then the student thinks about the word and has the option of writing the word again in the *think* column. In the last column, the student writes the word on the board. Then the student compares results. Another approach to spelling is to keep a spelling log as shown below (and in the next few pages) in the logs of Toni, Creston, and Sarah.

Exemplar Emergent

WRITE	THINK	CHECK
lIke	lick	LiKe
wen	win	when
kotch	Koytch	catch
so	saw	saw
anemals	anemals	animals
pled	puled	pulled

Rubric

Linguistic Structures/Conventions: "Saw" is the only word which is spelled correctly in the *think* column. The improvement from the *write* to the *think* column is impressive, despite the problems. In Toni's spelling log, the two problem words, "and" and "like," are not generally demanding.

Commentary

In many respects, emergent spellers show remarkable progress in their understanding of spelling conventions (and, at the same time, their phonemic awareness). Nevertheless, these samples are still at the beginning stages of spelling mastery.

TONI			
10/17	D - and	11/10	LC - like
	D		LAT - liked
10/23	ND	12/8	LOCT - liked
10/25	AD	12/19	L - like
11/10	ND	4/10	LICT - liked
	LA		LIC - like
	ANE	5/14	LIKE
11/16	AND	5/21	LIKE
11/18	ND		
11/28	AND		
12/1	AND		
12/8	AND		

Exemplar

R u b r i c

Linguistic Structures/Conventions: Five of the words are spelled correctly in the *write-think-check* response, and "turkey" and "catch" show improvement from *write* to *think*. Creston's spelling log is showing excellent progress with difficult words.

Commentary

This early speller is showing excellent progress. More words and difficult words are being spelled correctly.

	WRITE	THINK	CHECK
1.	lake	like	like
2.	trke	trkeu	turkey
3.	kaos	Basch	catch
4.	wet	went	went
5.	ot	to	to
6.	plad	pode	pulled
7.	so	saw	saw
8.	hof	have	have

CRESTON			
10/20	DRS - dress	11/14	BODM - bottom
11/3	DRS	12/7	BODUM
1/5	DRAS	1/12	BOTUM
1/23	DRES	1/19	BOTUM
2/18	DRESS	2/11	BOTOM
3/5	DRESS	3/18	BOTTOM
		4/2	BOTTOM
11/3	WCH - watch		
11/6	WACH		
1/8	WACHT		
1/12	WACHT		
2/11	WATCH		
3/6	WATCH		

Exemplar

WRITE	THINK	CHECK
1. little		
2. People		*little*
3. Wene	Whene / when	*people*
4. sleeves	sleeves / slevis / sleeveaves / slen	*when*
5. fancy		(*sleeves*)
6. Animles / animles	an mles / an im lal / anlmale / animals	*fancy*
		animals

Rubric

Linguistic Structures/Conventions:

- Fluent spellers have mastered such difficult words as "animals" (missed by a previous student), "sleeves," "everything," and "flowers."
- Both the spelling log and the *write-think-check* spelling sheet show the writers' remarkable growth as the student works through the spelling of new words.

SARAH			
11/3	AVVETAG - everything	11/6	SLLE - silly
11/6	AVVETAG	11/15	SALLE
1/31	EVERYTHING	11/17	SALEE
		12/7	SALEE
11/20	FLLAOWZ - flowers	1/3	SILLEY
	FLLAWRZ	3/15	SILLY
1/11	FLAWRS		SILLY WILLY
6/1	FLOWERS	3/26	SILLY

Commentary

The fluent student spells difficult words correctly and, at the same time, shows an increasing sophistication in the use of print to segment and analyze the flow of language. These rankings are based, in part, on difficulty of words attempted and percentage wrong. For example, Sarah (Fluent) may be struggling with more words than Creston (Early) or Toni (Emergent), but Toni appears to be limiting herself to simple words ("and" and "like"). The *write-think-check* approach to spelling gives the students the opportunity to edit their work and thereby practice various strategies for identifying letter-sound relationships. The *write-think-check* approach also provides a record of how students use invented spelling as a technical device for identifying segments in the flow of oral language. That is, students use print to segment the oral sounds and to recheck their work. With such a record, the teacher can analyze what students are doing. Below is one teacher's analysis of a student's spelling problems.

WORD	SPELLING	PATTERN
ULEG	ugly	unusual spelling, sounds represented but not sequenced correctly
SAND	stand	omitted one letter, consonant blend incomplete
GRAM	grab	consonant different
SURT	shirt	vowel letter different, consonant digraph (*sh*) incomplete
PLULE	pull	vowel letter added, sounds represented but not sequenced correctly
HANDE	hand	vowel letter added
WARE	where	vowel letter different, consonant digraph (*wh*) incomplete
WATES	wants	vowel letter added, consonant blend (*nt*) incomplete
PESET	pet	sounds represented but not sequenced correctly, vowel and consonant letter added

Teachers also use the miscue approach to examine patterns of sound in oral readings. Below are two examples of miscue analysis from an article by Wendy Hood:

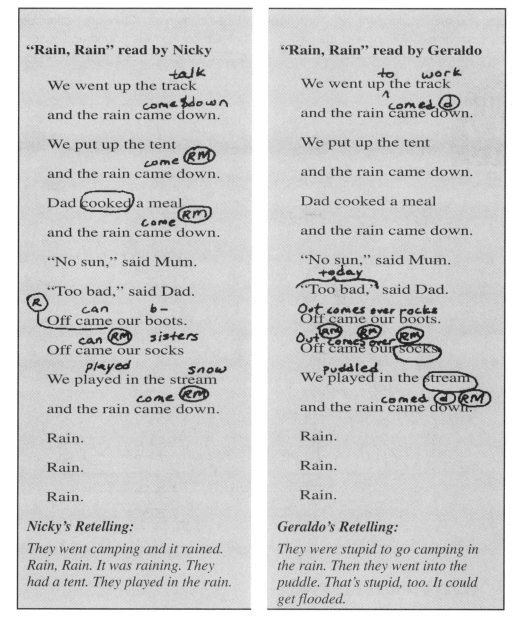

"Rain, Rain" read by Nicky

We went up the track

and the rain came down.

We put up the tent

and the rain came down.

Dad cooked a meal

and the rain came down.

"No sun," said Mum.

"Too bad," said Dad.

Off came our boots.

Off came our socks

We played in the stream

and the rain came down.

Rain.

Rain.

Rain.

Nicky's Retelling:

They went camping and it rained. Rain, Rain. It was raining. They had a tent. They played in the rain.

"Rain, Rain" read by Geraldo

We went up the track

and the rain came down.

We put up the tent

and the rain came down.

Dad cooked a meal

and the rain came down.

"No sun," said Mum.

"Too bad," said Dad.

Off came our boots.

Off came our socks

We played in the stream

and the rain came down.

Rain.

Rain.

Rain.

Geraldo's Retelling:

They were stupid to go camping in the rain. Then they went into the puddle. That's stupid, too. It could get flooded.

Teachers can evaluate how samples of miscue analysis represent levels of achievement in reading.

Connections to Standards

	STANDARDS											
Targeted	1	2	3	4	5	6	7	8	9	10	11	12
Supplementary	1	2	3	4	5	6	7	8	9	10	11	12

Students apply knowledge of language conventions such as spelling (6) to enable them to communicate effectively with a variety of audiences and for different purposes (4). By using the *write-think-check* strategy and by keeping spelling logs, students learn to use a variety of writing strategies (5).

Task

After studying the poetry of Dr. Seuss and talking about his use of alliteration, students in an ungraded primary classroom created alphabet books. They wrote alliterative sentences for each letter and illustrated their sentences. Students worked on the books in groups, but each took primary responsibility for some of the pages. Completed books were bound and shared during a Day for Young Authors.

Exemplar

Rubric

Cognition: This student needs the scaffold of lined paper to control writing.

Linguistics/Conventions: The student shows a good grasp of alliteration in the sentence. The first line seems off the mark.

Commentary

This student has created a simple sentence using alliteration with the letter "B." The student used lined paper to guide the writing and practiced writing letters before writing the sentence. The illustration is detailed and clearly depicts a "big boy."

Exemplar **Early**

The quilt man quilted a quilt.

R u b r i c

Cognition: This student does not need the scaffold of lined paper. The writer apparently has internalized the sensori-motor routines needed to maintain a straight line.

Linguistics/Conventions: This student attempts a difficult repetition (q). The drawing is not important to the author.

Commentary

This student has created a sentence which shows her ability to connect sound and meaning. Although the sentence is simple, the sentence illustrates alliteration through repetition of the word "quilt." The student shows a growing ability to manipulate language: she correctly uses "quilt" as an adjective, verb, and noun. The drawing clearly illustrates the sentence, but the drawing is not developed.

Exemplar

Rubric

Cognition: No need for scaffold of lined paper.

Rhetoric: Selects topic interesting to peers.

Linguistics/Conventions: The invention of the word "caterday" (for "Saturday") maintains the alliteration.

Commentary

This student has created a word ("caterday") which shows her ability to play with sound and meaning. She told her teacher that she invented the word "caterday" in imitation of Dr. Seuss's style of word play. Unlike the early and emergent exemplars here, this student began her sentence with a prepositional phrase rather than a noun subject. The reference to the popular singer Coolio suggests this is certainly popular within an audience of peers. The drawing cleverly illustrates the sentence and, to insure the audience recognizes Coolio, the student has incorporated a line from one of his well-known songs.

Connections to Standards

	STANDARDS											
	1	2	3	4	5	6	7	8	9	10	11	12
Targeted	1	2	*3*	*4*	5	6	7	8	9	10	11	12
Supplementary	*1*	*2*	*3*	*4*	5	*6*	7	8	9	10	11	12

In the creation of a class alphabet book based on the poetry of Dr. Seuss, these beginning readers and writers applied a wide range of strategies (3). For example, students drew on their prior experience (Coolio), their interactions with other writers (Dr. Seuss), and their understanding of textural features (alliteration). Students adjusted their written and visual language to communicate with an audience of peers (4). As students continue to read a wide range of literary and nonliterary texts (1, 2), they will develop increasingly sophisticated responses to print and nonprint texts (6).

Task

The students were asked to write sentences in response to informational books they had read.

Exemplar Emergent

Text

ieNoSTZXWVHABDENgQccMTZYPPBFDGGAaagzzTMFMSSWZ
YPe4DDBAVESaQMDABZWR.

Translation

Not known, but she role-played "reading aloud" with appropriate content and inflection when her class shared their stories.

Commentary

The student needs to continue writing, work on beginning reading, and to notice "real" invented spelling where sounds and letters are related. For instance, the teacher might sit down with her as she begins to write a story and help her sound out a few words. (Stories are a better place to begin for many students.) If the student wanted to start out a story with "My mother is nice," you could say "M-m-m-m-my. What letter does that sound like at the beginning?" and help her connect it to the letter name "m." Since this student's grasp on the names of the letters is still a little shaky, it might take her a while to be able to do this for herself.

Rubric

Cognition: The flow of letters may be increasing, but word and sentence sense may be weak or missing altogether.

Conventions: The student is not yet mapping letters to the sounds of oral speech.

Exemplar

R u b r i c

Cognition: The writer has some fluency in writing, but there are disjointed sections.

Conventions: The writer has some serious spelling problems. Sound-letter relationships are a problem in particular areas.

Text

King Kobrob or the king ov snacsw ol snacs or sbrog. FREE WILLY is the bast anoml

Translation

King cobras are the king of snakes. All snakes are strong. Free Willy is the best animal.

Commentary

This student needs lots of reading and writing. The teacher should watch for spellings of common words (*are, of*) to emerge and help this student develop strategies for finding words in reference books and elsewhere. For instance, the teacher might give the student a list of "five little words" to tape on his desk to refer to as he writes (updating once he's spelling those consistently), as well as doing a minilesson with a group of students or the whole class about the difference between finding words in a thematically organized word book and in an alphabetical dictionary.

Text

Keko is My Favoit Walse. Keko Lived in Mexacow Cide. He Mufte to Oregon.

Translation

Keiko is my favorite whale. Keiko lived in Mexico City. He moved to Oregon.

Commentary

This student needs lots of reading and writing strategies for finding words in reference books and elsewhere. The student may also need a minilesson on *ed* endings. For suffixes, the teacher could present a minilesson where children look at pairs of words like *move/moved*, *walk/walked*, and *want/wanted* (these examples include the three pronunciations of *ed*) and ask them what they notice. For proofreading, the student could be asked to pick three words from a piece that she thinks might be spelled wrong and see whether she can find them in a reference book or elsewhere in the classroom.

Text

> I Like dinosaur the dragon and the rhinoceros and the unicrn and the alligator And the hippopotamus and the leopard

Translation

> I like dinosaur, the dragon, and the rhinoceros and the unicorn and the alligator and the hippopotamus and the leopard

R u b r i c

Cognition: The writer is fluent in processing text.

Conventions: The writer has a few spelling problems but is developing methods of self-correction.

Commentary

This student used a picture dictionary to create this response. Therefore, the piece gives virtually no information about his development level. How a teacher should work with him would depend on what he or she saw in self-generated spellings. The student has apparently mastered the use of an important reference tool.

Connections to Standards

	STANDARDS											
Targeted	1	2	3	4	5	6	7	8	9	10	11	12
Supplementary	1	2	3	4	5	6	7	8	9	10	11	12

This task targets standards 1 and 4. Beginning readers and writers need opportunities to read and respond to a wide range of print and nonprint texts (1). When students write in response to reading or viewing, they learn to adjust their written language to communicate effectively with a variety of audiences and for different purposes (4). In this set of exemplars, students should also read and respond to a wide range of literary texts (2). As they gain expertise in reading and writing, students will apply their growing knowledge of language structure and conventions, media techniques, figurative language, and genre to create, critique, and discuss print and nonprint texts (6).

Task

The samples below come from a class in which students had the option of putting a letter in the classroom complaint box. Other teachers who have reviewed these samples have looked for ways these samples make visible the children's evolving notions about letter form. Some have described how they help students develop a sense of form by showing the students examples of letters and by highlighting parts (Dear _____; Sincerely, _____). A key point, which these samples illustrate, is that the argumentative form (in this case, a complaint letter) begins early and develops along with growth in narrative and other forms. Some assessments treated argument as a stage after narrative.

Emergent

Exemplar

Rubric

Rhetoric: Emergent papers do not have salutations and, sometimes, closings.

Language Structure/Conventions: Many serious errors. Unlike other letters, the emergent samples are often almost unreadable.

Commentary

This sample illustrating an emergent paper is actually the one with the most serious complaint. But the reader must translate "pockt" to "poked," "wit" to "with," and "pensl" to "pencil." In addition, the reader must unscramble "witapensl." The closing ("Hahnal") is out of place (pushed in at the second line because of lack of space), and the address to the reader is missing altogether.

Early

Exemplar

Rubric

Language Structure/Conventions: The early samples have serious word-level errors but the writer's sense of sentence structure is good.

Rhetoric: The salutation of the letter is usually missing in the early range.

Themes/Ideas: The focus of the ideas is sometimes not clear in early papers.

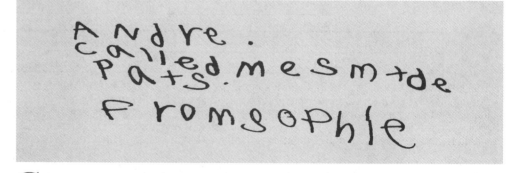

Commentary

This complaint letter does not have an opening salutation. It has the author's name as a closing, but is missing "Love" or "Sincerely," which appear in the fluent samples. This writer does add, "From." This early writer is developing quite well, but needs to begin to add some elaboration.

Dear Mrs.D Jeff Matt H.
and Aron ~~other~~ was
around the room. runing

Love Farnoosh

Dear Mrs G
Matt B. was prtebing
that he was dead
Love Kaley

Rubric

Rhetoric: The fluent complaint samples include an opening salutation and a closing.

Linguistics/Conventions: The fluent complaint samples have some serious errors (they are, after all, usually first drafts). But they have a good sense of sentence structure.

Commentary

The fluent complaint samples usually have a salutation and closing, ten or twelve words and a clear grievance ("Runing around the room," "Prtebing that he was dead"). The students show that they are beginning to develop fluency in their writing.

Connections to Standards

	STANDARDS											
Targeted	1	2	3	//4//	//5//	//6//	7	8	9	10	11	12
Supplementary	//1//	2	3	//4//	//5//	//6//	//7//	//8//	9	10	11	//12//

The targeted standards in this task are 4, 5, and 6. In writing these letters of complaint, students adjust their use of written language to communicate effectively with an authentic audience, the teacher (4). The letters show students using a variety of strategies as they compose (e.g., experimenting with salutations and closings) (5). The students have applied knowledge of language structure, conventions, and genre to create print texts (6). The supplementary standards in this task are 1, 7, 8, and 12. As students grow more sophisticated in this genre (argument), they may read about problems and propose solutions (1), conduct research on issues (7), gather information from a variety of sources (8), and construct written arguments for various audiences. Students can use this genre to accomplish their own purposes (12), such as influencing school policy or speaking out on issues of national concern.

Task

In several K–3 classes, the students were asked to write a description of or a story about someone the student knows. Drawings were acceptable as supplemental information but not required.

Exemplar

Rubric

Cognition: The student is learning to focus on a subject and to elaborate a subject. In both drawing and writing the student develops increasing control of pencils, crayons, and other school tools. The eye-hand motor coordination is steadily improving. The student is still trying to develop some fluency with the code.

Rhetoric: The narrator-subject relations are close. The student is developing recognition of audience as is evident in the frontal figures of the drawings.

Linguistics/Conventions: Letter-sound relationships are increasingly conventionalized, and words and sentences are increasingly segmented into units. Sentences are still line-at-a-time units. Periods are rarely or never used to mark sentence units.

Commentary

The student uses the printed alphabet to segment the flow of language and make the sounds of oral language visible, giving the student new control over the structure of language. The translation: "Someone means a lot to me. My friend Kelly. Plays with me a whole lot." The drawing helps focus the writing. In fact, the drawing becomes a source of ideas for writing.

Exemplar — Early

I have a frend named Daniel. he is frendly I like hime verey much. do you like him?

R u b r i c

Cognition: This student shows an increasing fluency with both drawing and printed text.

Rhetoric: This student addresses the audience ("Do you like him?"), showing a new step in rhetorical awareness.

Linguistics/Conventions: This student is beginning to use the conventions for ending sentences (periods, question marks). This is an important advance in beginning writing.

Commentary

This student has developed substantial fluency in the use of the alphabet to write words and sentences. Spaces between words, end punctuation in sentences, margins around writing—all of these features show a writer who may no longer need the drawing as a support or scaffold for the writing. In fact, the drawing has become in many ways an independent graphic, which illustrates the theme of the writing (Daniel), but is not essential pre-writing.

Exemplar — *Early*

Rubric

Cognition: These students show an increasing fluency with the code.

Rhetoric: These students use the "and—and" or "because—because" structure to elaborate details into story structure. These chains do not necessarily provide consistent elaboration.

Linguistics/Conventions: Sentence and word conventions and letters are increasingly under control. Spelling problems have decreased.

Commentary

These five young writers have begun to separate from drawing as a scaffold for writing, and, at the same time, they have increasing control over letter-sound relations and the use of language to segment oral language into words and sentences. The story structures are usually chains of "and—and" and "because—because." These chains provide elaboration, but the details seem to be just added on, as if a list were just under the surface.

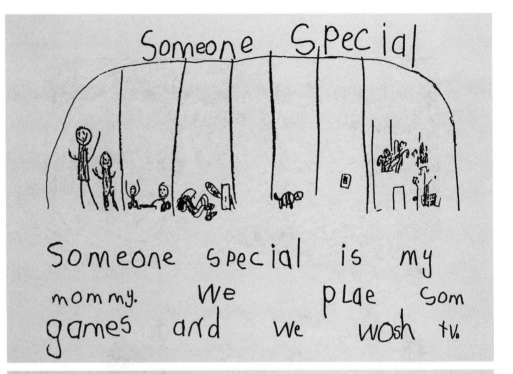

Someone Special

Someone special is my mommy. We plae som games and we wosh tv.

I Like to play with my dog. I Like my dog Becus he runs with me. mi dog licks me when I get home.

Sometimes my mom and dad do the same thing. Sometimes they do the apasit.

I love my Dad Be cus he loves me (and) Becus he thos the ball to me and Becus we plae weth hes bat.

mom an my Dad and my dog my cat my grand parents. my Kitts and my Frens.

Exemplar

Someone Special

I'm foursing my mom to make my own brecfast.

My mom is kissing me.

My mom is hug (huging) me.

My mom is special becase she kisses me and she hugs me and (she) ıe dusin't make me make my own brecfast but Sometimes (she can be a grouch.)

someone that means alot to me is my mom and dad. My mom helps me when I have trubls with wirds that I need. My dad helps me when I have trubls with number facks. I like it so much when my mom and dad helps me.

R u b r i c

Cognition: These papers have increased code fluency and use organizing strategies which go beyond chain sequences. The paper below, which introduces the idea of help and then provides two examples (Mom and Dad), appears to be using a comparison-contrast strategy for organizing the paper.

Rhetoric: The narratives of these students tend to move from one episode to another, but these two writers add a dual dimension, describing two characters (Mom and Dad) or two sides of one person (kisses and grouch) or I-help-her/she-helps-me (next page).

Text/Linguistics/Conventions: The titles in the top paper and next page are the first signs of formal text conventions. This paper also continues an interesting interaction of print and visuals. Spelling keeps improving, and sentences have end punctuation, usually periods. The paper below on this page has an excellent first sentence, showing the student's evolving understanding of "thesis sentence" and "focus." The paper on the next page and the paper at the top on this page are both using the title as a substitute for the thesis sentences. Many students, doubtful about how to provide focus in the first sentence, use the title instead.

23

Fluent Exemplar continued on page 24

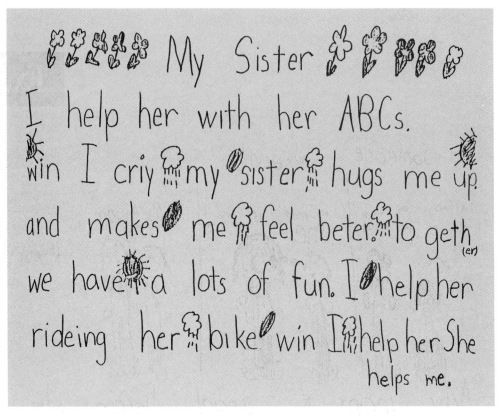

My Sister

I help her with her ABCs. win I criy my sister hugs me up. and makes me feel beter. to geth (er) we have a lots of fun. I help her rideing her bike win I help her She helps me.

Commentary

Previous papers used drawing to develop and scaffold a story, but fluent papers do not. Visuals here are decorative and illustrative. The story in "someone special" is a contrast of episodes (kiss, grouch) and a series of episodes: Kisses me, hugs me, [makes] breakfast. Then we find out she is a grouch. This first sample appears to be using both the typical "and—and" episodic structure and a comparison/contrast. The last two stories (Mom/Dad and I-help/she-helps) use a dual structure from Mom to Dad and from writer helping the sister to sister helping the writer. It concludes, "win I help her She helps me." These three fluent writers appear to have mastered the basic skills of narrative representation, to be experimenting with comparison/contrast representation, to have sensori-motor routines under control, to have mastered many problems of spelling and sentence structure, and to have learned to use details to develop a story.

Connections to Standards

	STANDARDS											
	1	2	3	4	5	6	7	8	9	10	11	12
Targeted	1	2	3	*4*	*5*	*6*	7	8	9	10	11	12
Supplementary	*1*	*2*	3	*4*	*5*	*6*	*7*	*8*	*9*	10	11	*12*

The targeted standards in this task are 4, 5, and 6. In writing about someone special, students adjust their use of written and visual language to communicate effectively with various audiences (4). Students make strategic use of written and visual language as their communicative purposes change (5). Students apply knowledge of language structure, conventions, and genre to create print and nonprint texts (6). The task also assesses 1, 2, 7, 8, 9, and 12 as supplementary standards. As students grow more sophisticated in this genre (description), they may read and respond to a variety of texts (1, 2), conduct research (7), and gather information from a variety of sources (8). Depending on the topic and focus, descriptive writing can help students develop an understanding of and respect for diversity (9), and to use language to accomplish their own purposes (12), e.g., enjoyment or the exchange of information.

Task

Students were asked to keep journals recording experiences both in and out of class. Frequent journal writing helps beginning writers develop fluency.

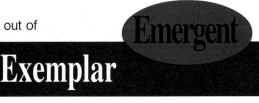

Emergent

Exemplar

ABET HE WOS WOKED PDST E

Commentary

Translation: *Robert. He was walking down the street.*

The student read his written message to the teacher. The student demonstrates **emerging awareness of the relationship between written and visual language.** The spacing after "rabet" indicates his sense of word boundaries is emerging. The letters used in the sentence correspond closely to the intended message.

Rubric

Cognition: The student is beginning to develop sensori-motor control, enabling him to position writing and drawing appropriately on page.

Rhetoric: The student used drawing and writing to communicate a brief message.

Linguistics/Conventions: The student forms letters correctly and the letters correspond to the words he intends to convey in the message.

Early

Exemplar

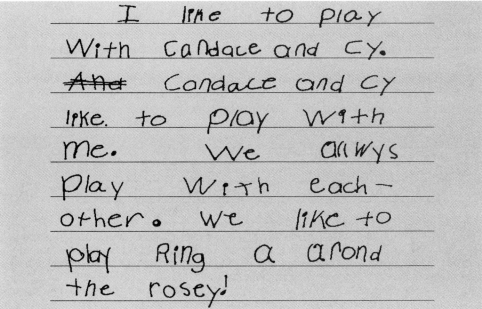

I like to play
With Candace and Cy.
And Condace and cy
like. to play with
me. We allwys
Play with each—
other. We like to
play Ring a arond
the rosey!

Rubric

Cognition: The student prints carefully and neatly, showing good sensori-motor control.

Rhetoric: Awareness of audience is shown in the careful composition of the sentences. The writing is a simple recounting of events, elaborated with few if any details.

Linguistics/Conventions: The student uses punctuation, capitalization, and spacing to indicate sentence and word boundaries.

Commentary

This student has conscientiously observed conventions of writing, perhaps at the expense of self-expression. The journal entry, however, clearly communicates a personal experience important to the writer.

Exemplar

Rubric

Cognition: The student shows excellent cognitive control of sensori-motor routines and awareness of total composition. Events are clearly sequenced and details are included.

Rhetoric: The student writes fluently about personal experiences for personal audiences.

Linguistics/Conventions: The student does not yet regularly use punctuation, capitalization, or spacing to indicate word or sentence boundaries; however, the fluent writing shows that the student has a clear sense of words and sentences.

Commentary

Translation: *"Last night we went to California Pizza and my sisters got Beany Babies. Sarah got a seal and Katie got a fox. I didn't get anything because there was nothing that I liked. When we went to Mexico I got a puppet. I also got a pop gun. When we went to California Pizza my Grandma came. I also got dessert and it was a chocolate sundae."*

This first-grader kept a daily journal while on spring vacation with his family. Only one entry is shown here. The writing is impressive for its organization and use of detail. This writer uses a sophisticated vocabulary. Spellings of challenging words are quite accurate.

Connections to Standards

	STANDARDS											
	1	2	3	4	5	6	7	8	9	10	11	12
Targeted	1	2	3	4	5	6	7	8	9	10	11	12
Supplementary	1	2	3	4	5	6	7	8	9	10	11	12

The targeted standards in this task are 4, 5, and 6. In writing journal entries, students adjust their use of written and visual language to communicate effectively with a close, personal audience (4). Students make strategic use of written and visual language as their communicative puposes change (5). Students apply knowledge of language structure, conventions, and genre to create print and nonprint texts. The task also uses 1, 2, 7, 8, 9, and 12 as supplementary standards. Students may use journals to respond to a wide variety of texts (1, 2), or as a research tool (7) as they gather information from a variety of sources (8). Journal writing can help students explore and develop an understanding of and respect for diversity (9). Students also use journal writing to accomplish their own purposes (12).

T a s k

The students were asked to fill out student-made library cards when they checked out books from the classroom library. These records provide an indication of the student's breadth of reading.

Exemplar — **Emergent**

Name of Book
Hideandseek
peAnut

	date out	date in
	1-24-97	
	1-30-97	
	1-3-97	
	3-3-97	

R u b r i c

Cognition: This student is beginning to select books for independent reading.

Linguistics/Conventions: The student observes some of the conventions of filling out a library card.

Commentary

This emergent reader is beginning to read for his own purposes. He has legibly recorded his use of two books and understands the purpose of the "date out" column.

Exemplar

R u b r i c

Cognition: The student regularly selects books for independent reading.

Linguistics/Conventions: The student has kept an accurate record of titles, dates out, and dates returned.

Commentary

This student's library card shows that she selects books regularly for her own purposes. The card shows that the student checked out twelve books between October and March. While this card alone gives us no information about the student's comprehension of the books listed here, it does suggest that she may be becoming a competent and responsible reader who may already be fluent.

Name of Book	date out	date in
Meet Addy	10-1	10-18
Amelia Bedelia	11-6	10-28
Tinky socks	11-1	11-6
Fox And His FRIENDS	11-13	12-18
The SuRpRise Party	12-18	12-6
Mollys Pilgrim	12-6	12-7
Amelia Bedelia	12-7	1-14
The Ghost in tent 19	1-14	1-20
The Teacher From	1-30	2-5
The Invisible dog	2-5	3-12

	d out	d in
The kids in Ms. calmarts class	3-4	4-15
Mrs. Jeepers is missing	4-15	

Exemplar

name of Book	date out	date in
AmeLIA BeDELIA	—	—
FeliCity Lerns a Leson	10-7-96	11-11-96
mR. Putter and Tabby Pick thePear	11-11-96	11-13-96
mR. Putter and Tabby Pick thePears	11-13-96	11-13-96
Fox on the Job	11-13-96	11-14-96
Fox in Love	11-19-96	11-19-96
AmeliA BeDeLIa-And The Box	11-19-96	
Sock's	1-7-97	1-20-97
Pippi LongStoing's	1-25-9?	2-27-97

(first row header shows: name of Book — example entry below it)
10-1-96 / 10-7-96

Name of Book	in	Out
Charlie and the Chocolate fatory	9-28-9?	2-24-9?
Germs, germs, germs	9-29-97	4-28-97
RiBSY		4-29-97

Rubric

Cognition: The student regularly selects books for independent reading.

Linguistics/Conventions: The student has kept an accurate record of titles, dates out, and dates returned.

Commentary

There is very little difference between this student's reading record (Fluent) and the preceding one (Early). However, there are a few clues to suggest that this student may be somewhat more fluent in some respects than the previous student. This student's card suggests that she reads thematically and purposefully on topics of interest. Her selection of genres shows some breadth and depth.

Connections to Standards

	STANDARDS											
Targeted	1	2	3	4	5	6	7	8	9	10	11	12
Supplementary	1	2	3	4	5	6	7	8	9	10	11	12

The students have selected books from a well-stocked classroom library which includes print and nonprint (e.g., picture books) texts, fiction and nonfiction, classic and contemporary works, and literature from many periods in many genres (1, 2). Wide reading invites students to apply a wide range of strategies to comprehend, intrepret, evaluate, and appreciate texts (3). As regular library users, students participate as knowledgeable, reflective, creative, and critical members of a literacy community (11). Students select books to accomplish their own purposes (12).

Task

K–3 students often study units on earthquakes, dinosaurs, food, and other topics. In this task, the teacher in an ungraded primary classroom read to the students a *Magic School Bus* adventure in which the bus traveled through the human digestive system. Students then worked in pairs to create a visual representation of the digestive system, attempting to capture critical information from the text.

Exemplar

Rubric

Cognition: Fluent graphic lines and printing.

Conventions: The graphic is not very clear. Is this a body?

Ideas: Ideas about the digestive system are scrambled.

Commentary

The students in this emergent sample have situated the digestive system within a vague outline of the human body. They correctly identified the epiglottis ("aipiglitis"), large and small intestines, and stomach as parts of the digestive system. But in the drawing, the stomach is misplaced. The drawing does not suggest how the digestive system functions or the interrelationships of its parts. Interestingly, the teacher stated that one of the students who worked on this drawing is one of the most fluent readers in the class. Students may not use visual and written language with equal fluency.

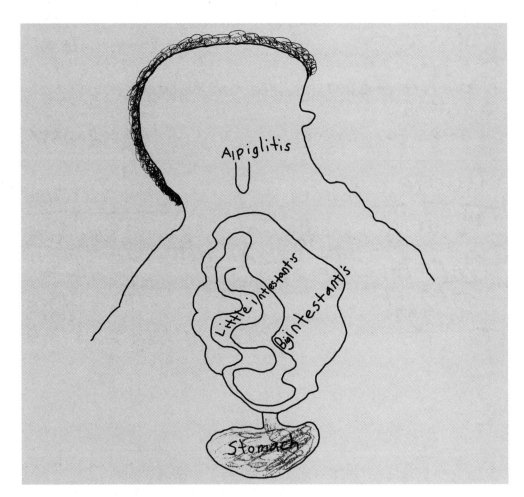

Task

Nathan described the assignment which prompted this piece as follows: "I was to read the book *Call It Courage* and take the information from the book and create my own book using social studies concepts." In other words, the student is asked to treat a literary text as a source of information illustrating social studies concepts—a transactional response to literature. Following are excerpts from Nathan's book, which includes visual representations, a conceptual list, a book summary, and an information summary.

Response to Literature (Transactional)

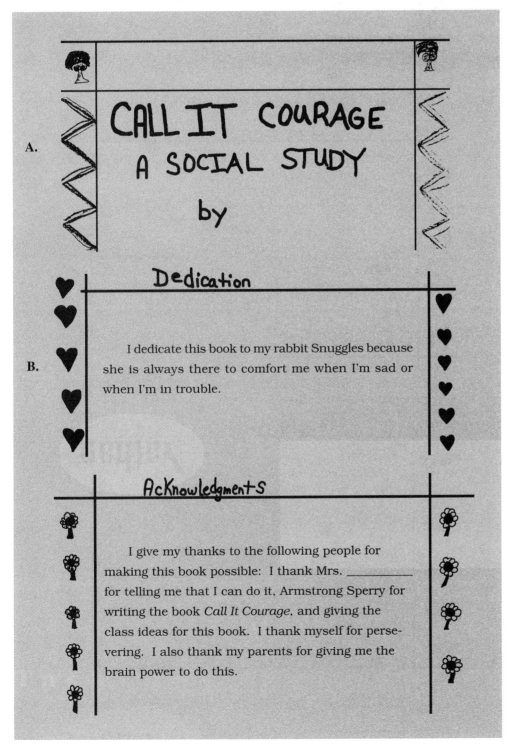

A.

CALL IT COURAGE
A SOCIAL STUDY

by

B.

Dedication

I dedicate this book to my rabbit Snuggles because she is always there to comfort me when I'm sad or when I'm in trouble.

Acknowledgments

I give my thanks to the following people for making this book possible: I thank Mrs. _____ for telling me that I can do it, Armstrong Sperry for writing the book *Call It Courage*, and giving the class ideas for this book. I thank myself for persevering. I also thank my parents for giving me the brain power to do this.

R u b r i c / C o m m e n t a r y

A. Shows awareness of the visual conventions and the print conventions of a picture story book, including title page, dedication, acknowledgements.

B. Uses language appropriate for audience and purpose.

Paper continued on page 90

Response to Literature *(continued)*

C. Groups information conceptually.
D. Uses writing and visual representation to demonstrate conceptual understanding.

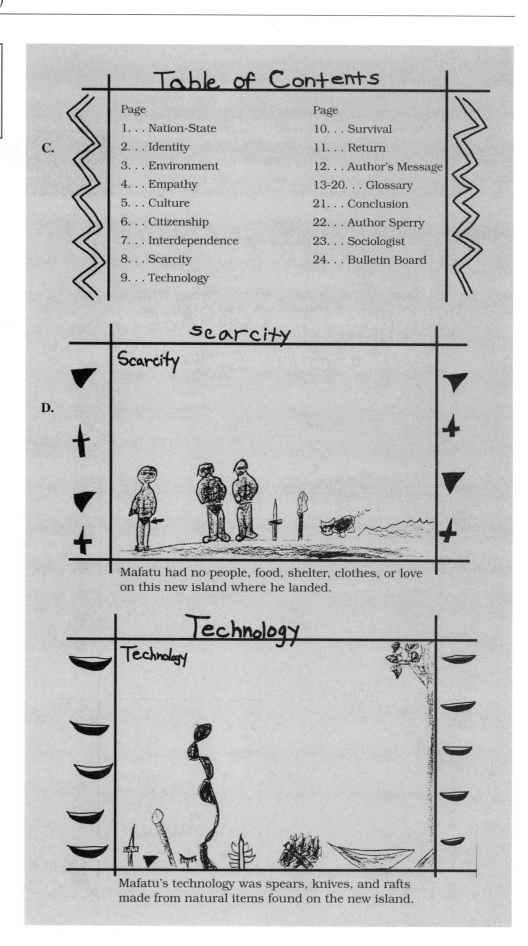

Table of Contents

C.

D.

scarcity

Scarcity

Mafatu had no people, food, shelter, clothes, or love on this new island where he landed.

Technology

Technology

Mafatu's technology was spears, knives, and rafts made from natural items found on the new island.

90

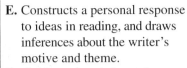

Author's Message

E. I think Armstrong Sperry's message from the book *Call It Courage*, was that you should always have hope within you, and to never give up when bad things are happening. He also had a few more messages. They were, that there is always a light at the end of a dark tunnel. Mafatu never had love or encouragement from his family. That's why he left to the dangerous island. I think Armstrong Sperry wanted to show that parents should pay more attention to their children.

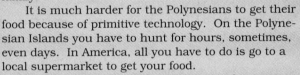

Sociologist's Conclusion

F. I, _____, have learned that the people of the Polynesian Islands believe in many different gods. Most Americans believe in one main God. Each member of an American or Polynesian family have their own responsibilities that make things better for the family.

It is much harder for the Polynesians to get their food because of primitive technology. On the Polynesian Islands you have to hunt for hours, sometimes, even days. In America, all you have to do is go to a local supermarket to get your food.

G. Unlike my family, Mafatu did not get love or encouragement from his father. If his father had been more loving to his son, Mafatu wouldn't have gone to another island and almost gotten killed. But then he may not have gotten his courage.

E. Constructs a personal response to ideas in reading, and draws inferences about the writer's motive and theme.

F. Connects new information to prior knowledge by contrasting the primitive and modern technology of food gathering.

G. Demonstrates understanding of complexities of the text.

Connections to Standards

Nathan demonstrates substantial achievement in:

• applying a range of strategies to comprehend, interpret, evaluate, and appreciate a text (3);

• applying knowledge of language structure, language conventions, and genre to create print and nonprint texts (6);

• using written and visual language appropriately to communicate effectively with an audience (4).

Writing in a Literary Genre: Fictional Narrative

High

Task

On the entry slip, Nathan writes that this piece began in fifth grade as a response to reading about Native American groups: "I had to choose one group and write a chart showing all of their aspects. Then I had to take these facts and make them into a fictional story in which I was the Indian in that time." In other words, Nathan was asked to give a poetic response (write fiction) to informational, non-poetic materials. Following is Nathan's narrative account.

Rubric / Commentary

A. Establishes setting and skillfully introduces main character.
B. Uses concrete language and sensory detail to develop character.
C. Creates conflict in the story.
D. Develops character by revealing narrator's thoughts.
E. Crafts chapter to leave reader in suspense.
F. Successfully resolves conflict with the bear.

Chapter 1
Early Life

A.   It was May 6, 1442, in the North Eastern Woodlands. The wind was blowing hard and the fire was burning hot. A new baby was born. The whole Algonquin tribe cheered. The baby was held up high in the air. Meanwhile, his mother sang a song to the gods. "Oh mighty gods give my baby a name that will suit him well.

Suddenly, there was a crack of lightening, then a white fox came running across the middle of the pow wow. "Then it is so, we will call you White Fox," she said.

As the years went by, I grew older. My grandfather told me stories about my native culture. Best of all, I met a friend, his name was American Eagle. When we were five we became best friends.

"I hope to become a good hunter and have a lot of adventures in my life," I thought to myself.

Chapter 2
Childhood

B.   As I got older, I met more friends, but my favorite friend other than American Eagle was Maui. I love the way her eyes twinkled and her hair was carried by the wind. Her beautiful brown eyes, and her gorgeous face make me melt. I noticed her when we were both 12 years old. Maui and her mother migrated from the Cherokee tribe.

C.   I have had a wolf as a pet since I was eight. We named him Roudy. Roudy and I would play hide and seek in the woods every day. One day a bear got angry and clawed at Roudy. It's claws caught Roudy's cheek.

D.   Roudy was bleeding badly. I took Roudy into a cave after ten minutes of running. I had no idea where we were. But the thing I did know was that we

E.   were lost and we weren't going anywhere because the bear was waiting outside, and it was getting dark.

Chapter 3
Teen Years

F.   The next morning I looked outside the cave. Luckily the bear was gone. I woke Roudy, and we walked out of the cave. Roudy's cut was heeling quickly. Suddenly, I heard voices. I quickly climbed a tree. Roudy hid behind a big bush The voices became louder and louder. I realized that the

G. voices were Maui and American Eagle. I jumped off the branch to greet them, but all I really did was startle them.

"Where have you been?" Maui yelled, "everyone's been looking for you."

I told them what had happened. Suddenly, I saw a nice group of rocks that could be made into arrows. Five minutes later I saw a group of sticks that could be made into bows.

H. Time passed very quickly. None of us knew where we were or how to get back. Maui, American Eagle and I were still all together. We were all around thirteen or fourteen, no one was keeping track of the days or months or even years!

I remember being very hungry. I decided to go catch some fish. When I got to the pond I started to fish. I was very successful. I caught ten fish. I was still hungry so I decided to try out my new bow and arrow. I crossed over mountains and farmland. I was very successful at hunting too, but it took me a while to track down that deer. I killed a bear and a deer. I kept doing this day after day. But one day, we were found by some hunters from our tribe. We were finally safe.

Chapter 4

Twenty - Death

I. As the years passed by, Maui and I became closer and closer. We got married. We had two kids. Their names were Little Bear and Little Deer. Maui cooked a great deer, and after I had told my story once or twice, Little Bear wanted to become a great hunter, and Little Deer wanted to become a dancer at pow wows. Little Bear, Little Deer, Maui, and I were all going to build a nice long house. American Eagle helped. Unfortunately Roudy died, but we did find another wolf in the woods, we called him White Spot. I was a great hunter, and Maui told children stories about the Algonquin culture.

One day while I was hunting I was attacked by two bears, luckily I got away alive, but I was badly hurt.

J.

TOMBSTONE

Here lies White Fox

Brave Warrior

1442 - 1482

Died of rabies

G. Introduces more plot complications.

H. Locates events in time.

I. Uses details (names) which suggest having read background histories on Indians.

J. Skillfully concludes story, leaving reader to fill in gaps.

Connections to Standards

Nathan demonstrates substantial achievement in:

- using writing to communicate effectively with a particular audience for a particular purpose (5);

- applying knowledge of language structures, language conventions, and genre to create a print text (6).

Task

Nathan used a variety of strategies in preparing to write the preceding story. For example, he created a time line of White Fox's life, a list of his vital statistics, and various drafts of the story. Below are two examples of pre-writing strategies Nathan used.

Commentary

A. Uses webbing to explore topics for writing.
B. Organizes concepts and synthesizes information read into two contrasting columns.

A.

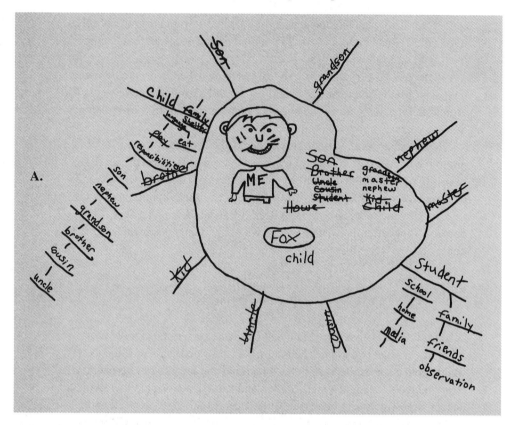

B.

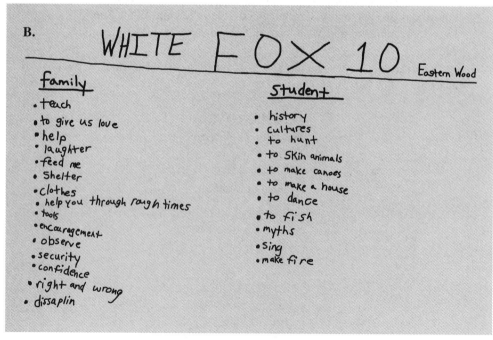

Task

Nathan's teacher certified that he had read the works listed below.

Breadth of Reading

Student Reading Record

NAME _____ GRADE 5

DATE	BOOK TITLE / AUTHOR	TYPE OF BOOK	HOW READ	RATING
	Say Cheese and Die / R.L. Stine	Mystery	Ⓐ G T	1 2 3 ④ 5
	The Baby-sitter / R.L. Stine	Horror	Ⓐ G T	1 2 3 4 ⑤
	The Whipping Boy / Sid Fleischman	Historical Fiction	Ⓐ G T	1 2 3 ④ 5
	Elie Wiesel / Michael A. Schuman	Biography	Ⓐ G T	1 2 3 ④ 5
	Say You're Dead / John Peel	Mystery	Ⓐ G T	1 2 ③ 4 5
	The Sun is on	poetry	Ⓐ G T	1 2 3 ④ 5
	The Family Under the Bridge /	fiction	A Ⓖ T	1 2 3 ④ 5
	The Séance / Jane Lowery Nixon	Mystery	Ⓐ G T	1 2 3 4 ⑤
	The Big Wave / Pearl S. Buck	Historical fiction	A Ⓖ T	1 2 3 ④ 5
	Call It Courage / Armstrong Sperry	Historical Fic.	A Ⓖ T	1 2 3 4 ⑤
	A Wrinkle in Time / Madelyne L'engle	fiction	A Ⓖ T	1 2 3 4 ⑤
	All It takes is practice	Realistic	Ⓐ G T	1 2 3 ④ 5
	I have a dream	Biography	Ⓐ G T	1 2 3 ④ 5
	Mrs. Frisby and the Rats of NIMH / Robert O'Brein	Science Fiction	Ⓐ Ⓖ T	1 2 3 4 ⑤
	Silent Witness / Carol Ellis	Horror	Ⓐ G T	1 2 3 4 ⑤
	The Giver / Lois Lowery	Science fiction	A G Ⓣ	1 2 3 ④ 5
	A Girl called Boy / Belinda Hurmence	Science fiction	Ⓐ Ⓖ T	1 2 ③ 4 5
			A G T	1 2 3 4 5
			A G T	1 2 3 4 5

For the date be sure to include the date started and the date you completed the book.

A= read the book alone G= read the book in a reading group T= the teacher read the book to the class

1= poor   2= fair   3= average   4= good   5= excellent

Rubric

The student was asked to present evidence that he or she had read:

- at least twenty-five books (or equivalent);
- a balance of literature and non-literary works;
- at least three different genres or modes;
- at least five different authors;
- at least four books focusing on one issue, writer, or genre.

Commentary

Nathan documents reading seventeen books, including a balance of fiction and nonfiction.

Documents reading in at least three different genres and five different authors.

Shows in-depth reading in science fiction.

List does not include informational reading for research project, *Exploring the Atlantic* (page 98) or *My Life as An Indian* (page 92).

Ratings show what engaged the reader, but he does not include total pages or plot summary.

Should have dated log entries to help the portfolio reader understand pace of reading.

Connections to Standards

Nathan demonstrates substantial achievement in:

- reading a wide range of texts to build an understanding of texts, of himself, and of the cultures of the United States and the world (1);
- reading a wide range of literature (2).

NATHAN'S PORTFOLIO

High

Reading Reflection

Rubric/Commentary

A. Describes reading for a variety of purposes, including pleasure.
B. Clearly explains reading strategies.
C. Evaluates self as a reader.

Connections to Standards

Nathan demonstrates substantial achievement in:

● participating as a knowledgeable, reflective, creative, and critical member of a literacy community (11);

● using language to accomplish his own purpose (12).

Task

In preparation for writing the reflective essay (page 85), the teacher asked students to write reflections on their reading.

When I read with a group I feel good. The reason I feel good is that when one of my classmates stumbles on a word I might be able to help them out, then I feel proud about what I have done.

A. Besides reading in school, I read magazines and mystery books at home. I really love to get scared when I read.

Besides reading for fun, I read because I am told to, or it is a suggested assignment. But I love to read all the time for fun but sometimes I read things that I don't enjoy anyway.

B. When I don't understand something I've read, I go back and read it over and over again until I understand the concept.

When I come to a word I do not know, I stop and sound it out until it makes sense to me. Although usually I do not stumble.

C. My progress as a reader this year has been that I have read many more books this year than I had in the past year or two.

Task

Nathan chose to include a poem in his portfolio.

Snow
(A crippled boy's thoughts)

A.

Snow flakes fall
Like feathers from a pillow
As they land on the limbs
Of a withering willow.

B.

Snow can be dangerous
Snow can be fun,
The snow has an enemy,
It is the sun.

Snow is dangerous
Because it turns to ice.
Snow can be fun
Because it tastes really nice.

Children love
To play in the snow,
They whimper and whine
When it's time to go.

The laughter of children
The winds freezing blow,
They have so much fun
With the snowballs they throw.

C.

I see the people sled
I see people ski,
Oh how I wish,
That it could be me.

D.

Rubric / Commentary

A. Skillfully uses rhyme (ABCB rhyme scheme).

B. Shows syntactic awareness in stanzas.

C. Adopts first person point of view and reveals narrator's thoughts.

D. Uses visual representation in an attempt to enhance reader's comprehension. The effort is not particularly successful.

Connections to Standards

Nathan demonstrates substantial achievement in:

● applying knowledge of language structure, language conventions, figurative language, and genre to create print and nonprint texts (6).

Report of Information

Task

Nathan read the book *Crystal* and then wrote an informational report on whales. Following are excerpts from Nathan's paper.

Rubric / Commentary

A. Engages reader by creating a scenario.

B. Skillfully links facts about whales and geographical facts.

C. Error in sentence structure reflects writer's attempt to use more complex form of expression.

D. Minor errors in conventions do not interfere with meaning.

E. Uses visual representation to demonstrate understanding and, apparently, to engage reader.

Exploring the Atlantic

A.   Imagine yourself swimming peacefully in the tropic waters of the Atlantic Ocean. You hear an eerie sound that echos in your ears. It is a humpback whale. Humpbacks are born in Silver Bank. Silver Bank is 700

B. square miles of ocean far south in the West Indies. The temperature is very warm, even on a winter day. Although if you swim north the water will become cooler. Once the humpbacks are born they go to Stellwagon.

C. Stellwagon is located in Cape Cod, Massachusetts. Stellwagon is a nursery for young calves, as well as a feeding ground for their mothers or other adults.

   After the humpback's stay at Stellwagon they migrate to Silver Bank

D. because winter is coming and the water is becoming very cold. The humpback whales hate cold and hot water so they migrate between seasons.

E.

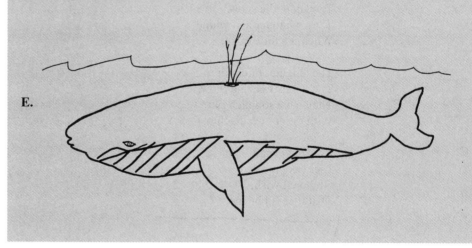

Paper continued on page 99

F. As a big gray humpback whale swim over top of you, you think that the whale must weigh more than six elephants. With a big splash the whale reaches the surface to take its breath of air. The humpback and all other whales must come to the surface to get a breath of air because it is a mammal.

G. Mammals need to breath air to live.

A young whale can grow to be thirteen feet long and weigh over a thousand pounds. To a whale the fluke is like a giant paddle. A fluke is the two halves of a humpback whales tail.

H. The nose of the humpback is on top of it's head. The nostril is called a blowhole. The blowhole is connected to the humpback's lungs, just as the

I. human nose is connected to the lungs. The humpback whale has several folds in it's skin. Only humpbacks have white long flippers. The lips close tight when the humpback whale dives under water. Baseball sized lumps in front of the blowhole are called tubercles.

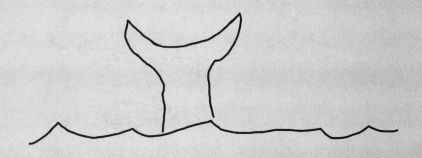

The humpback whales sing eerie songs that echo through the ocean water. While scuba-diving in the Atlantic Ocean, I observe that the hump-

J. back is now hanging motionless beneath the surface preparing to make it's song. I come to the surface of the water and ~~you~~ see a group of humpbacks resting on the surface of the water. This is called "logging."

I start to swim to my boat. The sailors pick me up and bring me aboard. I leave the Atlantic Ocean. Now ~~you~~ we are about one mile away from the groups of whales. Suddenly I see the blow of a humpback whale in the

K. distance. The Latin name for the humpback whale is "Megaptera Novaeangliae."

F. Recalls opening scenario.

G. Presents information logically (although facts about size of young whale seem out of place).

H. Supports main ideas with details.

I. Uses comparisons to explain unfamiliar concepts (e.g., fluke, blowhole, tubercles).

J. Maintains device of opening scenario, although mixing up "I" and "you."

K. Some lapses in organization. Why is Latin name given here?

Paper continued on page 100

L. This section shows numerous lapses in organization which Nathan might have avoided with webbing, outlining, or mapping (as in White Fox narrative).

M. Uses specialized vocabulary correctly.

N. Nathan seems to have abandoned organizational plan and begins listing random facts.

O. Observes conventions of research report.

L. A whale's pregnancy lasts one year. A humpback whale cannot lie on the ocean bottom for to long because it has to keep breathing air. A humpback whale feeds on different kinds of fish depending on where the humpback lives. Humpback whales look for little fish to eat. The singers are usually the male humpback whales.

M. The humpback whale's baleen is very important in it's life because it helps it catch food. The humpback opens it's mouth and sucks in fish and krill. The humpback holds it's prey in it's mouth and then lets the water run out through the baleen.

The mother provides milk for her calf. The humpback can drink up to fifty gallons of milk a day, that means three hundred and fifty gallons of milk a week. The humpback whale eats more than three thousand pounds of fish a day that is at least one million calories.

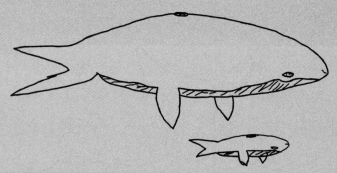

N. Finback whales are the second largest type of whale in the world. Finbacks are among the fastest, so they are called the "grey hounds of the sea." Finbacks are the only mammals known to have such uneven color on their bodies. finbacks lower jaw baleen is white on the right side, and black on the left side. A finback's spout goes straight up fifteen to twenty -five feet high.

Toothed whales swim in tight family groups called pods, such as the humpback whales. The growths on the right whale's head are called callosities. Whales float when they die.

Orca's are a group of whales that are the humpback's enemy. The orca's attack in groups.

The blue whale is the biggest animal since the dinosaurs.

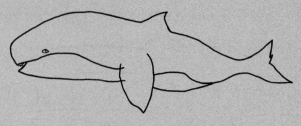

BIBLIOGRAPHY

O. Smyth, Karen C. Crystal: The Story of a Real Baby Whale. Stoughton, Massachusetts, Alpine Press, 1986.

"Whales." The World Book Encyclopedia. 1992 edition.

Task

The students were asked to collect information from several sources and to outline this information.

HUMPBACK WHALES

12-8-94

I.   Environment
A. Tropical waters
B. 80 degrees waters
  ✓1. Humpback whales are found in the tropic waters of the ocean
  ✓2. Two thousand humpbacks go to Silver Bank to have thier babies.
  ✓3. Silver Bank is 700 square miles of ocean far south in the West Indies.
  ✓4. Water temperature is about 80 degrees even on a winter day.
  ✓5. Water becomes cooler when Crystal swims south.
  ✓6. Stellwagon is a nursery for these young calves as well as the feeding ground for their mothers and other adults.

II.   Appearance
A. Humpback Whale, weighs more than six elephamts.
  1. is an air breathing mamal
  2. Crystal is only the size of his mothers flipper.
  3. Crystal is nearly 13 feet long, and weigh over a thousand pounds.
  4. Flukes are like a giant paddle
  5. Largest animols ever to have lived on earth

Commentary

Nathan closely followed this outline for the first paragraph of the report. His check marks indicate facts he included in the first paragraph. His use of the scenario ("Imagine yourself . . .") in the final draft reflects his personal engagement with the text read.

Paper continued on page 102

Section III of outline shows some confusion about purpose of outlining but demonstrates his ability to use the form.

6. Crystal's mother weighs more than six elephants.
7. Front legs become flippers, rear legs dissapear.
8. Nose is on top of head.
9. Nostril is called a blowhole.
10. Only humpbacks have long white flipper
11. Humpbacks have several folds in their skin.
12. The blowhole is connected to their lungs.
13. Lips of the blowhole are shut tight when the whales dive under water.
14. Bringing your head above the surface slowly is called "skyhopping."

III. Interesting Facts
   A. Swim in pairs or groups
     1. When humpbacks breathe air their is a cloud of spray from the blowho
     2. Little humpbacks spout twice whe they dive deep.
     3. Males hang motionless beneath the surface.

Life
1. A whale's pregnancy lasts one year.
2. Can't lie on ocean bottom because they have to keep breathing air.
3. Humpbacks feed on different fish, depending where they live.

Task

The students were asked to include drafts which show evidence of revisions. The revised paragraph below became the last paragraph of the final piece.

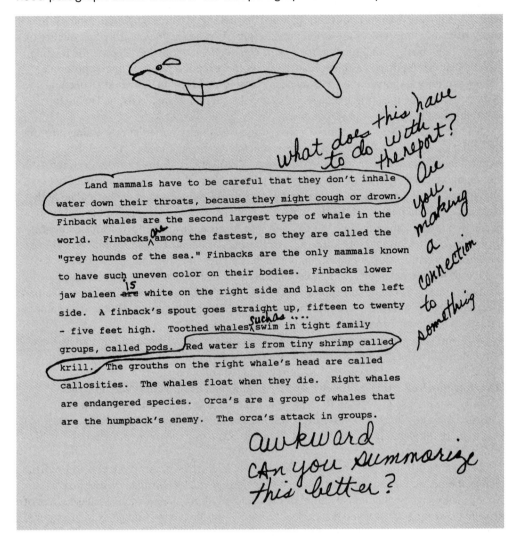

Commentary

The final copy of this draft paragraph appears on page 100. Note how Nathan responded to his teacher's questions and suggestions in the final draft.

Connections to Standards

Nathan demonstrates substantial achievement in:

● employing a wide range of strategies as he writes and using different writing process elements appropriately to communicate with a particular audience for a specific purpose (5);

● using informational resources to gather and synthesize information and to create and communicate knowledge (8).

Summary Commentary of Nathan's Portfolio

Nathan's portfolio shows he has attained a substantial level of achievement in the English language arts. Nathan has excellent encoding skills. His reading and his writing exhibit adequate mastery of conventions, such as spelling, usage, and punctuation. While some errors are noticeable, they are not distracting. In reading, the quantity and quality of evidence (e.g., background reading for *Call It Courage*, the humpback report, the reading list) suggest that Nathan is a fluent reader who comprehends a range of age-appropriate literary and informational texts. His teacher certified that Nathan delivered an accomplished performance: having read a well-balanced selection of materials, he is able to communicate the gist of what he has read.

The artifacts in Nathan's portfolio also suggest that he is skilled at processing information and uses a variety of strategies to understand and represent ideas. He sketches, outlines, brainstorms, uses visual representation, drafts and re-drafts. His letter of introduction and the excerpts from entry slips also demonstrate that Nathan is aware of his reading and writing processes, can set and achieve specific goals, and can articulate both strengths and weaknesses. Nathan's portfolio contains several examples of his ability to locate, manipulate, and translate information into forms appropriate for various audiences. For example, "Invention: Not Hot Pots," "Exploring the Atlantic," and "White Fox" have very different patterns of organization, but each is appropriate for audience and purpose. In "Exploring the Atlantic," Nathan demonstrates that he can conduct research using various sources. Although this report exhibits some overall lapses in organization, Nathan effectively varies sentence structure and length, usually creating linkages among sentences and paragraphs with appropriate transitions.

The portfolio pieces show that Nathan writes for a range of close and distant audiences, including a formal audience (the invention commercial), the reader of his portfolio ("Dear Reader"), a young reader of picture books (*Call It Courage*), and his own reflective self ("Reading Reflection"). Likewise, the portfolio pieces show that Nathan writes skillfully about close ("Reading Reflection") and distant (*Call It Courage*) subjects. Nathan also writes in a variety of forms: reflective essay, response to literature, book report, short story, and poems. He reads and responds to a wide range of materials, as his reading list suggests.

Nathan's portfolio selections show that he is conversant with key concepts in English such as theme, plot, character, and point of view (e.g., *Call It Courage,* "White Fox"). Some entries suggest that he is beginning to consider cultural ideas, such as quests, rites of passage (*Call It Courage*), and difference ("Snow"). In the poem "Snow," Nathan experiments with seeing the world through the eyes of another.

Overall, Nathan's portfolio demonstrates that he has a high level of declarative knowledge (*knowing that*), which enables him to read and write fluently; procedural knowledge (*knowing how*), which enables him to read a broad range of texts and write in a variety of genres; and background knowledge (*knowing about*), which enables him to perform well at almost every task he has undertaken for this portfolio. While a reader of this portfolio can easily perceive ways in which Nathan might improve his reading and writing even more (e.g., read texts in more critical and evaluative ways, eliminate usage and spelling errors in final pieces, set more specific literacy goals), Nathan's work is unquestionably in the high range of performance.

Portfolios

Nathan

Mandy

Daniel

Mandy's Portfolio

At the end of her fourth-grade year, Mandy compiled her portfolio representing a selection of the work she completed over the course of the school year. We have selected only a few pieces for inclusion here. Some of the pieces are excerpts only.

Reflective Essay (letter)

Task

Following is Mandy's introductory essay, written in the form of a letter addressed to the portfolio reader.

Rubric / Commentary

A. Describes writing process for favorite piece.
B. Clearly explains criteria for good writing.
C. Clearly explains criteria for being a good reader. (Mandy included an audiotape in her original portfolio as evidence of her fluency in reading.)
D. Assesses strengths and processes in reading.

Connections to Standards

Mandy is developing skill in:

• adjusting her use of written language to communicate effectively with a specific audience for a particular purpose (5).

> Letter of Reflection
>
> Dear Reader,
>   I hope you enjoy looking through my portfolio. I worked very hard on it all. I worked especialy hard on my story titled, "The Case of Pitton's Castle". It took me about a month and a half. I had to type it up once then reprint it three more times because I found mistakes. I am very proud of it.
>   My tape tells how good of a reader I am. I think I am a good reader. I can read pretty fast and pronounce words well also.
>   My reading logs show how much I read each day and if I understand what I read. Each day I like to tell one or two things that happen. Sometimes even more. I also like to read a variety of books. Once and a while I get into ruts with books. You'll see that in my reading logs.
>   Most of the time I liked doing this. I've put a lot of hard work in my portfolio. I think you will like it!
>   Sincerely,

A.
B.
C.
D.

Task

Below are excerpts from the "flip book" Mandy created in response to reading *Mr. Popper's Penguins* by Richard and Florence Atwater. On the entry slip for this "book" Mandy wrote, "It shows I understand what I read, and I can also write about it. I think this piece shows that there are other ways to write about a book than sitting down and writing an essay."

A.

Characters: Mr. Popper, Mrs. Popper, Janie, Bill, Captain Cook, Greta, Mr. Greenbaum, Admiral Drake, and all the baby penguins are the characters.

Rubric / Commentary

A. Identifies major characters.
B. Identifies the conflict in the story.
C. Identifies the major events in the story.

MANDY'S PORTFOLIO

B.

Problem: The Problem is Captain Cook gets sick so Admiral Drake sends Greta. The Greta has 12 babies! Mrs. Popper is worried about money.

C.

Action: One of the actions is they flew all around the U.S.A going to theaters to perform.

Paper continued on page 108

D. Uses visual representation to enhance text.

E. Identifies resolution of the conflict.

F. Makes an evaluative judgment about the text, but does not interpret or analyze text by showing us a general theme.

Connections to Standards

Mandy is developing skill in:

• applying a range of strategies to comprehend, interpret, evaluate, and appreciate texts (3);

• adjusting use of written and visual language to communicate effectively with a specific audience for a particular purpose (4);

• applying knowledge of language structure, language conventions, and genre to create print and nonprint texts (6).

D.

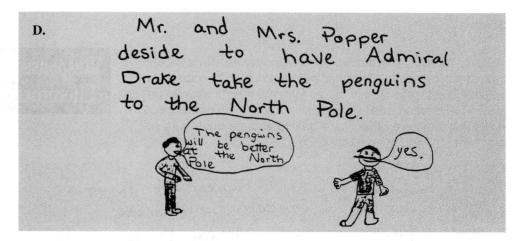

Mr. and Mrs. Popper deside to have Admiral Drake take the penguins to the North Pole.

The penguins will be better at the North Pole

yes.

E.

Outcome: The outcome is Mr. Popper decides to go to the North Pole with Admiral Drake and the penguins.

Mr. Popper was here

F.

Opinion: I really liked this book. It's really funny. My favorate part was when the repair man came to fix the refrigorator.

Task

On the entry slip for this piece, Mandy states, "We studied the solar system in science and had to write a report. I used several resources. It's clearly written . . ."

Report of Information

A. Comets

Halley's comet is probley the best known comet. Halley's comet apears every 77 years as it orbits the sun It was seen as early as the year 240. Halley's comet last apeared in 1986. Most people only see Halley's comet once in a lifetime.

B. Comets dont apear very often when one does; it may be seen night after night. A comet has a head and a tail. The tail can strech for millions of miles. A comet can only be seen when it comes close to the sun. The sun lights

C. it up. A comet that apeared in 1844 looked like it had six tails!

A comet is formed by dust and small chunks of frozen ice. A comet goes around the sun. A comets tail normally points away from the sun. Bright streaks in the sky are actully comets or meteors. The sun warms the comet and and it turns into

D. gases. The gas makes the tail

E. glow so It looks like fire.

F. 1. Comets, Meteors, & Astroids - David J. Darling

G. 2. World Book - 1987

3. Comets - Fraklin Watts

4. Look Around Space - Margret Holland

Rubric / Commentary

A. Shows evidence of getting information from what was read.
B. The sentences are choppy. Sentences can be combined through subordinations and conjunctions.
C. Errors in spelling are noticeable, but don't interfere with meaning. Repeated misspellings of "appear" should have been corrected during editing.
D. Ends abruptly.
E. Lacks evaluative, analytic, or reflective judgments about the reading.
F. Uses a range of resources.
G. Attempts to create a bibliography.

Connections to Standards

Mandy is developing skill in:

• gathering and synthesizing data from a variety of sources (7);

• communicating her discoveries in ways that suit her audience and purpose (7).

Task

Mandy presented her comet report to the class in an oral presentation. Below is the teacher's evaluation of the speech.

Connections to Standards

Mandy is developing skill in:

• adjusting her use of spoken language to communicate effectively with a specific audience for a particular purpose (4).

Oral Report Evaluation
4th Grade

3	2	1
Good, strong voice, speaks loudly and clearly enough for audience to hear	O.K. voice, some what difficult for audience to hear	Very soft voice, difficult for audience to hear
Good eye contact with audience, looks at audience at least 5-8 times	Some eye contact with audience, looks at audience 2-4 times	No eye contact with audience
Knows and can pronounce all vocabulary associated with topic, can fluently give report	Some mispronunciation of vocabulary words associated with topic, may stumble over words	Cannot pronounce many vocabulary words associated with topic, may re-read or ask for help
Good expression	Some expression	No expression
Able to clearly express ideas to the extent that audience can respond	Somewhat confusing information, some difficulty in expressing ideas to audience	Cannot relate information to audience, audience cannot respond

Very good (handwritten annotation next to eye contact row)

Students will present an oral report and will be scored according to the above criteria. Required number of points - 10.

Total points _15_

Written by   6/94

Nicely given! (handwritten annotation)

T a s k

On the entry slip, Mandy writes, "In reading we read a story about making things in nature. I used drafts, conferences, and made corrections. I included a self-reflection. I told every step. I had fun making my corn husk doll. I hope I can teach other people to make one too!"

A.

> How To Make A
> Corn Husk Doll
>
> This is how you make a corn husk doll. You will need: Corn husks, water, a bucket clothe, a hot glue gun, sissors spanish moss, and a black marker. First you need to soak the corn husks in water. When they're wet they're easyer to form. Next you need to make the head. Pick 2 or 3 peices of corn husks a wrap them around your thumb so the ends hang down at the same length. With a small peice of corn husk tie right below you thumb in a knot. After that take a large husk and roll it up, the bend in the center and tie in the middle of that, you should tie both ends also. Those are the hands stick them in the slot below the head. Now you need a waste, so take a small corn husk and tie below the arms. Once you have that done you need to make a dress Get five or six husks and wrap them around the waste. Again get a small peice of corn husk and tie them around the waste If you want you can make pants. Split the legs apart with a sissors, and tie small husk around the bottem of the legs for the ankles. Now you can add hair, clothe or anything you want to your corn husk doll.

B.

C.

D.

R u b r i c /
C o m m e n t a r y

A. Clearly presents focus of paper.
B. Shows minor errors in word choice and spelling.
C. Uses appropriate transition words and phrases organizing the steps of the procedure ("first," "after that," "now," "again").
D. Explains each step clearly with concise language.

C o n n e c t i o n s
t o S t a n d a r d s

Mandy is developing skill in:

• applying knowledge of language structure, language conventions, and genre to create print texts (6).

Task

Mandy was asked to include a draft of at least one paper which was later finished. Below is a draft of the narrative explaining a procedure.

Commentary

Draft shows how Mandy revised list of materials needed and rearranged sentences for clarity. Numbered steps in draft to verify steps in procedure.

Connections to Standards

Mandy is developing skill in:

• employing a range of strategies as she writes and using different writing process elements appropriately to communicate with a specific audience for a particular purpose (5).

How To Make A Corn Husk Doll

① Here is the materials you will need: Corn husks, water, hot glue, a bucket for the water, sissors, clothe, markers, spanish moss, and newspapers.

This is how you make a corn husk doll. ② First you need to soak the corn husks in water. ③ When they are wet they're easyer to form. ④ Next you have to make the head. ⑤ Pick out two corn husks and wrap them around your thumb so the ends match and are about the same length. ⑥ With a small peice of corn husk tie right below your thumb in a knot. ⑦ After that take a large husk and roll it up, then bend in the center and tie in the middle of that, you should tie both ends and the middle. ⑧ Those are the hands, stick them up in the slot below the head. Now you need a waste. To do this so take a small corn husk and tie below the arms. ⑨ Once you have the done you need to make a dress. ⑩ Get five or six husks and wrap them around the waste. ⑪ Again get a small corn husk and tie it at the waste. ⑫ If you want you can make pants. ⑬ Split the legs apart with a sissors and tie a small string around the bottom of the legs for ankles. Now you can add anything to make your cornhusk doll the way you want it.

Task

Mandy's short story, "The Case of Litton's Castle," is a lengthy mystery in the style of Nancy Drew. On her entry slip Mandy wrote, "In language we have writer's workshop. This gives us a chance to write stories. I chose to do this myself . . . I typed it up several times to get it just right. I used drafts. I worked very hard typing my story, it took me a month and a half almost to finish it." To conserve space, the editors have deleted large portions of the story. Although many episodes of the intricately constructed plot do not appear here, the reader can still get a feeling for how Mandy handles plot, character, and theme.

Writing in a Literary Genre: Short Story

THE CASE OF LITTON'S CASTLE

A. "We really get to go to Litton's Castle?" asked twelve year old Beth Arnie.

"Yes, I guess we do. I just got an invitation from my niece, Carol. She owns the place," said Grandfather Arnie. "She heard you and your brother Kenneth are pretty good mystery solvers! It sounds like she has a mystery in store for you! It says here that strange things have been going on, and she needs your help to figure out what's wrong."

"When are we leaving?" asked eight year old Kenneth.

B. "Well," replied Grandfather, "I was planning on leaving around noon or so tomorrow. It's a four hour drive to Litton's Castle you know."

"We better start packing Kenneth, we only have twenty-four hours before we leave," Beth said as she and her brother ran up the stairs.

C. Noon came fast the next day. For Grandfather Arnie it did, but not for Beth and Kenneth. Every minute seemed like two days to them. But finally they were all getting into the car.

Four hours later they were all standing at the big oak front doors of Litton's Castle. Carol greeted them with a friendly "hello." She led the way into a dining room which had one long large table and a picture of a guy on the wall.

"Who is that?" asked Kenneth.

"That is William Litton," Carol told them, "He is the man that had this castle built in 1841. In his will he asked if that picture could remain there for all times. And we respected his wish!"

Grandfather Arnie looked puzzled. "Carol I understand you know the whole story of the Litton family, don't you?"

"Yes I do. Would you like me to tell you it?" Carol responded. Grandfather, Beth, and Kenneth nodded their heads. "Well, let me see, oh yes,

D. William Litton was a very wealthy man. For his wife, Lisa he had this very castle built for their twelfth wedding anniversary. After living in this castle for two years they had a boy named Winford, but they called him Winnie for short. Winnie was seventeen when Lisa Litton died of alcohol poisoning. Three years later William died in his sleep. In his will he gave everything to his beloved son. While Winford was away at college he trusted his loyal

Rubric / Commentary

A. Introduces the setting and major characters in the story.
B. Observes conventions of writing dialogue and uses dialogue to advance plot.
C. Skillfully manages passage of time.
D. Provides background through narration by one of central characters.

Paper continued on page 114

E. While some exposition is a bit far-fetched, Mandy clearly understands the conventions of the genre.

F. Develops plot with complications and conflicts.

G. Uses short sentences to advance action and heighten suspense.

H. (To conserve space, a large portion of the mystery was deleted by the editors.)

I. Heightens suspense with series of actions and quick transitions.

E. servant Gertrude, the maid and cook, to look after the house. When he came back he married Martha Black a girl he met while he was away. Gertrude wouldn't let them get married so Winford fired her for he felt it was the only way he and Martha would ever be able to get married. After they got married they hired another housekeeper because Martha wasn't too good in the kitchen. This wasn't any trouble because people would pay a fortune to even step foot into the castle. Four years after Martha and Winford married they had a son name William II in memory of Winnie's father. Winford and Martha were both shot in the back when William II was sixteen. In their will they asked to be buried in the cemetary that Winford's parents were buried in, but they were buried before the will was found. Now it is said that they were so mad that every night at exactly 12:00 they will come up to the castle and haunt it until 1:00 a.m. I've never seen the haunting but I've heard it."

"That's horrible!" Beth cried, "But how did you get the castle?"

F. "I met William II in college. We became extremely good friends. On the last day of college he asked me to marry him. I said yes, of course! But a week later he said he was moving to Russia and would have to cancel the wedding. But he asked me if I would like to buy Litton's Castle. I was delighted in the fact that I would have a chance to buy this castle and sad at the same time because I wouldn't be able to marry him. Well enough of that. Let me show you to your room. I gave you each your own room. They look out across the ocean. Sometime if it's nice enough I could take you for a ride in my motorboat."

G. Beth awoke with a jump that night. As she looked around the room she saw a pair of eyes right beside the bookcase. Beth was eager to see who it was. . .or what it was. She crept out of bed with only the moonlight to guide her path. After she had gotten two or three steps away from the bed the eyes disappeared into the darkness. "Mmmmmm," she said to herself, "that sure is strange!" But she was too tired to worry about that now so she jumped into bed and quickly fell asleep.   . . .

H. *[The characters undergo several adventures, including an encounter with and escape from a group of robbers. In the final scenes, the characters discover a secret room and solve the mystery]*

I. "That door. Lean against it!" commanded William II. Carol, Beth, Kenneth, and Grandfather Arnie pushed with all their force against the wall.

Paper continued on page 115

Very slowly the door began to open. It squeaked and creaked very loundly causing all of them to cover their ears. Carol, William II, Beth, Kenneth and Grandfather pushed it harder to make it go faster. When the wall stopped creaking they ran inside to find a small office with ripped chairs, a desk well covered with dust, a small file cabinet, and a book shelf. "This was my grandfather's privat office that nobody new about," William explained. He pointed to a name plate on the front of the desk. Then he went over to the file cabinet and started pulling out files.

"William! What are you doing?" Carol exclaimed.

"I'm looking for a certain file," he replied.

"Well, good luck!" Kenneth said, "It might be just a tad bit hard considering there about one hundred files in there."

"Found it," William said tossing a folder onto the desk. Kenneth was shocked.

"What is the name of the file?" Grandfather Arnie asked.

"Well, these are the blue prints of the castle. They might just tell us where the vault is!" William sounded proud of himself.

"Oh William, you are a genius!" Beth cried.

J. "Let's take these down to the kitchen and look through them just in case our friends show up!" laughed William II. He lifted a board and a staircase revealed. The rest of them looked at each other in surprise. "Watch your head!" he called. "We're coming to a tunnel." Afther they had gotten through the tunnel William lifted a board, and a stream of light shone down on them. He crawled out with everyone following.

The group decided they needed a bite to eat. They all followed William through another passage way that they had no idea about. It led into the living room. Near the fireplace the floor boards came loose. Now the nine detectives were taking his or her turn out.

K. With Beth's help Carol was able to fix them a delicious meal of hamburgers, corn, tomatoes, and potato chips. Right in the middle of their meal Ralph's head stuck out the secret entrance William had show them. The police noticed and grabbed Ralph's hands before he could escape.

Five minutes later both the two robbers were being led into the back seat of the squad car.

L. "I never could have done any of this without any of you!" Carol cried. Tears trickled down her cheeks.

We solved both the mysteries!" Kenneth added. "Let's celebrate!" Everyone agreed with him. . . .

J. Successfully resolves conflict.
K. Skillfully uses a variety of sentence structures.
L. Shows control of conventions.

Connections to Standards

Mandy demonstrates substantial achievement in:

● adjusting her use of written language to communicate effectively with a specific audience for a particular purpose (4);

● applying knowledge of language structure, language conventions, and genre to create print texts (6).

MANDY'S PORTFOLIO

Breadth of Reading

Task

The following excerpts show Mandy's reading during two nine-week periods. Mandy read a number of mysteries and challenged herself with *Little Women*.

Rubric/

The student was asked to present evidence that he or she had read:
- at least twenty-five books (or equivalent);
- a balance of literature and non-literary works;
- at least three different genres or modes;
- at least five different authors;
- at least four books focusing on one issue, writer, or genre.

Commentary

Mandy's reading record, from mid-January to mid-March, indicates that she read nine books or their equivalent. If she maintained this pace throughout the year, she would have come close to meeting the twenty-five book requirement.

List does not reflect a balance of fiction and nonfiction (reading for Comet report, page 109, is not in-cluded here).

Has read in-depth in one author and one genre.

Brief summaries under "What's Happening Now?" demonstrate comprehension and appreciation of texts read.

Book Title Drew	Date	Pages	What's Happening Now?
Nancy Ghost Stories / The Ghost Jogger	1-16-95	20 / 95	Nancy meets an old sailor named Pete and they find an old ship where two men are holding two kidnapped children.
The Bungalow Mystery	1-18-95	15	Nancy and Helen meet Laura strange gardians. They investigate a bungalow.
The Bungalow Mystery	1-20	19	Nancy comes home to see Hannahs broken leg. She wakes up in the middle of the night a sees somebody opening a window!
The Bungalow Mystery	1-25	55 because of Basic Skills	Nancy was about to solve the mystery when she got trapped in a secret wall with a man.
The Bungalow Mystery	1-26	39 Basic Skills	They capture Laura's gardians and find out they arent her real ones.
The Hidden Window Mystery	1-30-95	45 Iowa Basic Skills	Nancy learns about a hidden window that is missing she goes the Richmond to find it.
The Hidden Window Mystery	2-1	21	Nancy get knocked over the head and is now unconsuse!
The Hidden Window Mystery	2-3	15	Nancy is taking lessons from a famous artist. She is learning who knocked her out.
The Hidden Staircase Mystery	2-7	30	Nancy and George fall through a trap door. Bess sees a ghost. She knows Toy Hall is haunted
The Hidden Staircase Mystery	2-8	19	Nancy and George learn of two suspects The follow a peacok out into a field.

Paper continued on page 117

Book Title	Date	Pages	What's Happening Now?
The Hidden Window Mystery	2-9	19	Nancy catches Luke Deendly and he coffesses he was the one scaring them.
The Tripple Hoax	2-15	20	Nancy and Bess and George go to New York to try to figure out who stole their Aunts friends money.
Olga Korbut	2-20	13 pages are longer	Olga tries and tries the new moves. She get frustrat Nobody likes her moves. They say there dangerous!
The Page Master	2-22	12 pages are longer	Richerd, Fanstacy, Horror and Adventure are tring to get out of the library.
The Tripple Hoax	2-23	16	Nancy and Bess, and George go to a magic show. When they ask for the audience to particapate. They don't want George to help them.

Book Title	Date	Pages	What's Happening Now?
The Tripple Hoax	2-21-95	22	Nancy and Beth and Goerge go to Mexico City. When they are in a taxi someone comes along and side swipes
The Tripple Hoax	3-1-95	19½	Nancy's friend's grand-daughter was kidnapped by the Hoaxters. Nancy is doing all she can to find her.
The Tripple Hoax	3-2	17	Nancy and Bess and George learn that the hoaxers took Doloros to Los Angelas. They want $100,000 dollars
The Tripple Hoax	3-3	19	Nancy and Bess and George go to L.A. They rented a car. They almost got arested because somebody put dimond in the trunk. Then their car is stolen.
Little Women	3-8	5 we only had 13 min. and the pages are alote longer	Beth tells a story of how she went to the Fish Market and saw Mr. Larene give a fish to a hungrey old won

MANDY'S PORTFOLIO

117

Connections to Standards

Mandy is developing skill in:

• reading a wide range of literature and nonfiction (1, 2).

Book Title	Date	Pages	What's Happening Now?
Little Women	3-9	11 pages are longer	Jo goes to visit Laurie, because he is sick she tries to cheer him up. She tells him to visit them any time.
Little Women	3-10	11 pages are longer	Mr. Larence lets Beth use his grand piano. She makes him slippers for a thanks and he gives her a piano.
Little Women	3-13	7½ pages are longer	Amy bys limes at the store and gets in trouble at school. She has to throw out her limes and Mr. Davis slaps her.
"	3-15	10 "	Jo will not let Ami go to the movies so Ami burns Jo's favorate book. Jo says she will never forgive An
Little Women	3-17	7 "	Meg goes to a party and marmee sends her a note and Laurie sends her flowers.
The Clue In The Shadows	3-20-95	12 I didnt get started right away	Strange jokes are happening around the house. Mr. Boddy knows who is the joker.
"	3-21	30	Mrs. White, Prof. Plum, Miss Scarlet, Mr. Green, Col. Muster take a drive in Mr. Boddys car after he tells them not to.
Little Women	3-22	19	Laurie invites the March girls to go on a trip in the moutains with him. They go and have lots of fun.

Task

Mandy was asked to include a report on a place (a description) in her portfolio. Compare this brief account to "The Case of Litton's Castle," written later in her fourth-grade year. The difference shows Mandy's growth in writing.

The Mall Of America

A.   This summer my family went to to The Mall OF America. It took four hours to get there. The Mall Of America has four floors.

B.   It has a park in the middle called Knotts Camp Snoopy. In the park there was a roller coaster, a log chute, Mini golf, bumper cars, and a Yellow Flying

C. Eagle. There were more rides but I cant rember what they were. I hope

D. we can go there again.

Rubric / Commentary

A. Establishes context for account.
B. Lists facts she remembers.
C. Uses typical strategy of developing writers: "There were more but. . . ." Prewriting activities might have led to a more substantial piece.
D. Closes appropriately.

Connections to Standards

Mandy is developing skill in:

• applying knowledge of language structure, language conventions, and genre to create print texts (6).

Summary Commentary of Mandy's Portfolio

The entries in Mandy's portfolio suggest that she is making progress toward reaching adequate levels of achievement in English language arts. In reading, Mandy demonstrates adequate encoding skills. Mandy's reading record and responses to texts show she is a fluent reader who comprehends the gist of what she reads and makes some attempts at interpretation. Her writing is, for the most part, fluent. Her progress in writing fluently may be seen by comparing the early "Mall of America" piece to "The Case of Litton's Castle," written later in the school year. She demonstrates appropriate control of word choice and syntax. Errors in spelling and punctuation in finished pieces such as "The Case of Litton's Castle" and "How to Make a Corn Husk Doll" are minor and do not cause confusion about meaning.

The artifacts in Mandy's portfolio suggest that she is developing skills in processing information but uses a limited repertoire of cognitive strategies for understanding and representing ideas. In response to *Mr. Popper's Penguins*, Mandy produced a "flip book," which identifies the main characters, settings, major conflicts, and solutions. This piece illustrates Mandy's ability to comprehend and summarize the text. "Comets" shows Mandy's ability to gather and synthesize information through reading several sources. "The Case of Litton's Castle" demonstrates Mandy's ability to transform information gained through reading Nancy Drew's mysteries into an original, lively, and engaging story. However, there is no clear evidence in these entries that the student makes evaluative, analytic, or reflective judgments about literature read, or that she makes connections to broader issues and ideas.

Mandy's portfolio pieces show that she is developing skill in adapting her writing for a range of close and distant audiences (e.g., *Mr. Popper's Penguins* "flip book" for younger readers, "The Case of Litton's Castle" for peers and Nancy Drew fans, and "Dear Reader" letter for portfolio readers). Her portfolio selections show that she writes more skillfully about close subjects ("How to Make a Corn Husk Doll") than distant ones ("Comets").

Mandy's reading records reveal that she has read nine books during two nine-week periods, four informational texts for the comet report and two books in response to literature. The books represent at least ten authors in four genres: mystery, horror, fiction, and nonfiction. The evidence suggests she is a fluent reader who rarely tackles challenging literary or informational texts. While Mandy appears to be a competent and confident reader, she needs to go beyond a literal interpretation of the text read.

Overall, Mandy's portfolio demonstrates that she has a high level of declarative knowledge (*knowing that*), which enables her to read and write fluently. However, she is still learning how to put that knowledge to use (*knowing how*). For example, her writing often follows a formulaic approach (e.g., "The Case of Litton's Castle," response to *Mr. Popper's Penguins*). There is not sufficient evidence to conclude that Mandy reads a broad range of challenging texts, interprets or evaluates the texts read, or writes skillfully in a variety of genres. Clearly, though, she has mastered the structure and rhetorical devices of Nancy Drew mysteries. Mandy's portfolio places her work in the middle range of performance. It provides a good foundation from which she can expand her repertoire of skills, strategies, processes, and products.

Portfolios

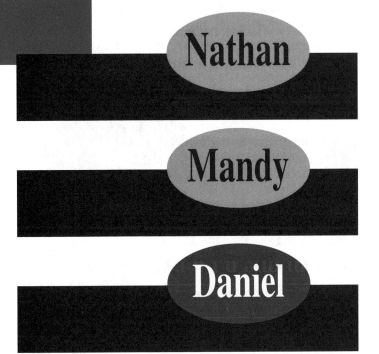

Nathan

Mandy

Daniel

Daniel's Portfolio

Daniel compiled this portfolio at the end of his fourth-grade year. His portfolio represents a selection of the work he completed over the course of the school year. We have selected only some pieces from Daniel's portfolio for inclusion here.

Reflective Essay — **Low**

Rubric / Commentary

A. Understands his effort and growth in assigned reading.
B. Identifies "best pieces" but does not explain choices.
C. Shows awareness of criteria for good writing.
D. Evaluates his speaking skills.
E. Reflects on his growth as a listener.
F. Reflection is difficult to read in parts.
G. Noticeable errors in conventions occur here and there and continue throughout the portfolio.

Connections to Standards

Daniel needs to show substantial improvement in:

• participating as a knowledgeable, reflective, creative, and critical member of a literacy community (11);

• using spoken, written, and visual language to accomplish his own purposes (12).

Task

Following are Daniel's reflection pieces in which he describes and assesses his growth as a reader, writer, speaker, and listener.

Purpose: The purpose of this reflection piece is to identify the growth you have made over the past year.

Using your portfolio, personal experiences and feelings as tools, describe your strengths and weaknesses in these areas:

READING

A. I think my Dear Mr Henshaw Journal is the best reading asdtement in 4th grade because I had t write a boud that book and if I dident I'd get a onit. I dont like reading because it is boring to me. I improved on reading because I got better grade in 4th than 3.

WRITING

B. I think my best pecies of writing is the sora letter, rockoy dangerus days, the rissing bird, my fatisy I like wrighting because I can get all my ideas out and shore them. my writing has improved by making more sense in the

C. story.

SPEAKING

D. I think my speaking log from Readers theaders is my best speaking, I got a + wo because i dident Read lines eluently, it was to soft. I did good q + speaking loud anuf.

LISTENING

E. I think my lisining logs from the Insect Reports in Nov. are my best lising in 4th grade because, I got a 3 on it. I think it is specil because

F. it is the best listinig thing I did, because it was the only listenog thing

G. in my portfol,e6.

Task

Following are excerpts from Daniel's journal written in the form of a letter addressed to the journal reader.

A.

R u b r i c / C o m m e n t a r y

A. Uses appropriate and effective illustration (note attention to perspective in drawing).

B. Shows awareness of seeing things from the character's perspectives.

C. Needs to support his interpretation with more details.

D. Appreciates humor in language.

E. Still needs to develop clarity in encoding ("poot" is "put," "rote" is "wrote").

April 74, 1995

dear reader,
    I started a book called dear Mr Hanshaw.

B. So far it is intresting because i can poot me in

C. Leigh's shoues. So far I think that Mr Hanshaw is geting annoyed because leigh keeps wrighting to him.

D.   I thought it was funny when He rote De Liver De letter De sooner De better De later De letter

E. De madder I giter. I thought that nothing else was funny.

Paper continued on page 124

F. Expresses opinion regarding the reading text.
G. Draws upon prior experience to comprehend and interpret text.
H. Knows importance of making personal connections to text.
I. Continues encoding problems ("also theys pages I cant relat to enything.").
J. Makes personal connection to text.
K. Shows the skill of prediction in reading.

Connections to Standards

Daniel needs to show substantial improvement in:

• applying a wide range of strategies to comprehend, interpret, evaluate, and appreciate texts (3).

---

tusdax April 7-5,1995

Dear reader,

F.
I thought it was intresting to Now more about Leigh bots. In the Questions of cource. I thought it was funny when His mom said TV rotins your brains. I also thought some of the Questions were boring. this time I cant compare

G.
His life to mine. exept when He sais I am a reguler kid.

Wednesday, April 26, 1995

Dear reader,
this time I read up to page 44. this time there was nothing funny to me. on pages 31-44 we found out a new caricter mr Fridly. He's

H.
the one who puts the flags up in school.

I.
also theys pages I cant relat to enything.

thrsday 3 1993

Dear reader,

Leigh finaly got an alarm on his lunch bat ther is nothing to relate to

J.
and no prodictions I think it was a good idea to get an alarm because it will catch the thefe. I thought the alarm was cool because I worted with paperiks

K.
and pubs. I prodict that will katch the thefe

Task

This piece, written in the form of a letter to a friend, is Daniel's response to the book *Sarah, Plain and Tall*. The handwritten piece below is the final copy, and the typed draft on the next page shows how Daniel responds to editing suggestions.

3/24/95

Dear Robert,

A. I read a cool book called sarah, plain and tall. there are four carictors in the book. these names are sarah, Caleb,

B. Jacob and Anna. the story is toled from Anna's point of view. my faxit part of the book is ch 3. I chose that chapter because sarah goes down to the prairy that day to see if sarah will

C. mary Jacob. And to see if sarah will be Caleb and Anna's mom.

before

she

came they wrote letters to each other. they wrote Questions like do you sing, do you snore. they also wrote Questions like can you keep a fire on at night.

the

story

D. took place on the prairy and in maine. the story is historical fiction. It is a really good book you should read it. I started a book

E. called Farmer Boy I will tell you about that in my next letter.

Sincerely,

F. p.s. you can look it up in the library.

DANIEL'S PORTFOLIO

Task

Students were asked to include evidence of drafts and revisions. In this case, Daniel typed the first draft of his Response to Literature.

Commentary

This draft shows that Daniel corrected some surface errors in the final copy (e.g., changes "kan" to "can"; capitalizes book title, *Farmer Boy*). However, in the final draft new errors are introduced that do not appear here (e.g., "prairie" becomes "prairy"; doesn't consistently capitalize first word in sentence).

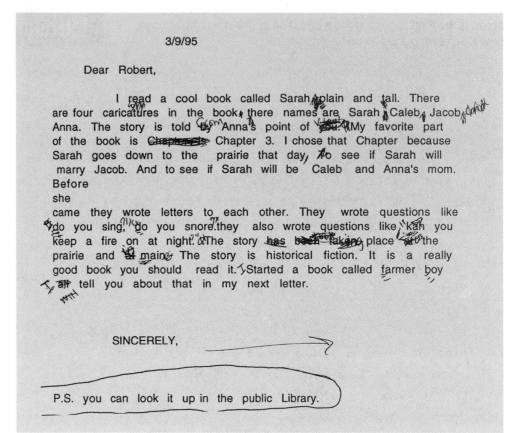

3/9/95

Dear Robert,

I read a cool book called Sarah plain and tall. There are four caricatures in the book, there names are Sarah Caleb, Jacob, Anna. The story is told by Anna's point of view. My favorite part of the book is ~~Chapter is~~ Chapter 3. I chose that Chapter because Sarah goes down to the prairie that day, To see if Sarah will marry Jacob. And to see if Sarah will be Caleb and Anna's mom. Before she came they wrote letters to each other. They wrote questions like "do you sing," "do you snore." they also wrote questions like "kan you keep a fire on at night." The story ~~has been taking~~ place at the prairie and at maine The story is historical fiction. It is a really good book you should read it. Started a book called farmer boy I all tell you about that in my next letter.

SINCERELY,

P.S. you can look it up in the public Library.

Task

Students were asked to use notes to gather information from different texts, to group that information into categories, and to write a report of information.

Rubric/ Commentary

A. Uses adequate visual representation.

B. Shows awareness of some of the conventions of report writing.

the world
of spiders!

A.

[drawing of a spider]

B.

I. table of contents
   what spider eats
   were spider lives

II. Desciacon of spider

III. Intresting facts about spider

IV. bibleography

Paper continued on page 128

DANIEL'S PORTFOLIO

C. Does not try to establish an over-all thesis sentence bringing to-gether paragraphs 1, 2, 3, and 4.

D. Groups information into con-ceptual categories in different paragraphs.

E. Gathers and summarizes infor-mation from reading texts.

F. Attempts to engage readers with questions.

G. Attempts to synthesize infor-mation gathered.

H. Uses comparison to describe spider's appearance.

I. Numerous errors in sentence structure and spelling interfere with reader's understanding.

What spider eats

C. Spiders eat small bugs like ants. I.t it katches it's food by traping it, in It's

D. web. Some spiders like trap door spiders It catches it's food by when the bugs

E. goes over it it, getsit. the Some thing withthe watter spider. Acsept the water spider lives under watter. spiders mostey eats grashopers. because it jampes

F. in its web Did you know that a Garten kind of spider paunses on its wictem.

Were spiderer lives
Did you know that spiders can live anywere
Spiders can live on webs. oron the watter. or in a hole. or in a haus e. or in a tree. they can even live in a closet.

G. eny were you hardly go or never went.

Descripcion of spider tere are meny diferent kinds of spiders. some are black Some are brown. like the black widow, it

H.

I. is red and black it has fur like a bare.

Paper continued on page 129

128

J.

I ntersting facts oboat spiders
Did you know Spiders
thred is thiner than a hair.
Or that more than 50
babsen in a egg. read this you
will findoat more, Spiders have
eaght igs. Spiders arnt incets
they are aractnids. beause
they have 8 legs. icets
have 6 legs. there sack the ble
of there wictems

K.

Biblography   11/21/94
Hogner childs Dorthy. spiders. New
york; Doubleday & compeny, 1959.
L AVI ne A. sigme d. Spider world. New
york; Dubel day & campeny, 1968.

L.

Shadels worik, shsen. the story of
spiders. Newyork. Dublday Campen94.

Writing in a Literary Genre: Fictional Narrative

Task

Daniel wrote "The Harmonica" in the middle of October, 1994. He creates some simple characters and events in his story. Although the whole story is not cohesive and comprehensible, Daniel uses supportive details to elaborate the events in his story. In addition, he began to show awareness of the conventions of a short story (e.g., he indicates four chapters and each introduces a different plot in the story).

Rubric/Commentary

A. Gives story an appropriate title.
B. Introduces the setting and characters.
C. Tries to engage readers.
D. Creates a plot.
E. Indicates a new chapter.
F. Demonstrates understanding of chapter structure and function.
G. Creates lapse in narrative by introducing self as character.
H. Shows awareness of having read other fictional narratives.
I. Ends abruptly and predictably.

A. 10/19/95 The Harmonica

B. Once a kid named Bob was walking to his friend Alexa's house. on his way he found a harmonica. So he played it. it became dark. So he went home. after that Alex called my mom the fence. Bob's friend said "come over my house" Bob said ok. so he went on his way

C. he plaed it. this is when the storyrilly begins. this time he disapperd. to Japan. he was in a Japaniese saeti

D. littel did he know that something bad was going to happen to him.

E. (ch 2.) one night he was going to watch the stars. when a littel women came up to him and gave me a witches scull. after she gave it to him. she dissepierd then he droped. It and ran into a tent. that was a probelem because that wasn't his tent! (ch 3.) that when he Met peter. peter let him slepe here for two days. on the secont day I was looking

G. for watter when I fored the harmonica. then I plaed it me and bob disepered, on a huge peach (ch 4) then I saw

H. a kid named James. this is when I plaied it.

but this time all three of us disepered. then I whent home and went to bed.

I. They used it to go home.

Task

The story, "Rocko's Dangerous Day," written in January, 1995, shows Daniel's growth as a writer. He has developed skill in engaging readers (e.g., "Little did he know that Spunky was flying over his head."). Also, this piece demonstrates his better understanding of the conventions of writing (e.g., indentation, skipping a line between paragraphs, using the format of dialogue).

Writing in a Literary Genre: Fictional Narrative

LOW

A. 1/25/95 Rocko's dangerus day

Once Rocko and his dog Spunky were going to
B. the beach. When they got there Rocko was planying in the sand when he called. "Spunky"
C. He looked every where. Little did he know that Spunky was flying over his head.

D. He saw his dog. He ran to katch him when he tripped over a rock. After he got up and ran as fast as he could. Rocko asked every wone at the beach. then he bumped into a famus star
E. EAth worm Jim.

F. Eorth worm Jim said "who are you looking for" Rocko said "My dog" "What dous he look like" "Well he's wite and black" "I seen him once in a fish store" Across the beach. So he went in. Spunky
G. wasint there (two weeks latter) Rocko whent to the grocery store. in Ile 12 were fish were. soon anuff
H. Spunky was there! So they whent home en went to bed

Rubric / Commentary

A. Attempts to engage reader interest with title and opening paragraph.
B. Introduces the setting and main characters.
C. Engages readers.
D. Introduces complications in plot.
E. Introduces a new character.
F. Develops a dialogue between the characters.
G. Informs readers of the passage of time.
H. Has a logical resolution.

Connections to Standards

From October to January, Daniel has made noticeable progress in:

• applying knowledge of language structure, language conventions, and genre to create print texts (6).

Substantial improvement is still needed.

Summary Commentary of Daniel's Portfolio

The entries in Daniel's portfolio suggest that he needs to show substantial improvement to reach adequate levels of achievement in English language arts. Most of the pieces are brief, indicating that Daniel possesses fragmented and sketchy understandings of texts. He does attempt to analyze and interpret texts read, but his analysis and interpretation are limited and simple. All pieces presented in the portfolio show that Daniel needs a significant amount of help in order to become an effective reader and writer.

Frequent and distracting errors in basic conventions throughout the portfolio suggest that Daniel has difficulty processing the language. The brief and superficial journal in response to the book *Dear Dr. Henshaw* suggests that he has a limited and generally literal understanding of what he reads. An exception is his research paper, "The World of Spiders!" which suggests that Daniel can construct a competent summary of texts he reads. However, there is limited evidence to indicate that he is a fluent reader. If records of reading, such as a log of books read, had been included, we might have had a better idea of the quantity and challenge level of texts Daniel can read.

The artifacts in Daniel's portfolio suggest that he lacks skill in processing information and that he may not be aware of strategies he might use to better understand and present ideas. For example, his entries in the *Dear Mr. Henshaw* journal show that he is aware of reading processes (e.g., making personal connections to texts) and strategies (e.g., predicting), but he does not apply reading strategies effectively. Daniel's letter of reflection indicates his interest and progress in writing, "My writing has inproved by making more sense in the story." Indeed, his later pieces confirm Daniel's effort and progress in writing (e.g., "The Harmonica" and "Rocko's Dangerous Day"). However, Daniel revises and edits haphazardly, if at all—processes that could improve his writing significantly.

The portfolio pieces shown here were written for a limited range of audiences: the *Dear Mr. Henshaw* journal shows Daniel's personal responses; "The World of Spiders!" "Rocko's Dangerous Day," and "The Harmonica" were written for young readers. Although most pieces show attempts to engage reader interest, the strategies employed are simple and predictable (e.g., "Did you know that Spider..." for the spider report; "Once a kid named Bob..." from "The Harmonica"; "Once Rocko and his dog Spunky..." from "Rocko's Dangerous Day"). In addition, Daniel writes in a limited range of forms: journal, personal letter, report, and fictional narrative. The observable improvement across the three fictional narratives suggests that Daniel has benefited from repeated attempts at writing in this genre.

Overall, Daniel's portfolio demonstrates that he has a low level of declarative knowledge (*knowing that*). His reading and writing are not yet fluent. The lack of variety among the artifacts in the portfolio (even though a variety of artifacts was required by the portfolio program in which he participated) suggests that Daniel's procedural knowledge (*knowing how*) is also at a low level. Similarly, there is little evidence to suggest that Daniel has drawn on background knowledge (*knowing about*) in order to produce the pieces shown here. That is, Daniel's lack of experience with a variety of genres of reading and writing probably contributes to the overall poor quality of his portfolio pieces.

Daniel's case raises interesting questions. How can Daniel be supported in continuing his progress in writing fictional narratives? How can his knowledge of this genre be used to improve his writing in other genres? What books might Daniel read that would build upon his interest in adventure stories and fuel an interest in reading? To what reading and writing strategies should Daniel be introduced to help him become a better reader and writer? How can his talent for visual representation be used to support other modes of representation? Daniel's portfolio exemplifies the low range of performance, but his work also suggests that he has an interest in becoming a more skilled reader, writer, and language user and that he has some knowledge and skills upon which to build. The key may be his engagement with topics he likes (spiders, adventure).

Conclusion

The *Exemplar Series* is the third part of the NCTE standards project: (1) *Standards for the English Language Arts* (NCTE/IRA); (2) the *Standards in Practice* series and the *Standards Consensus* series; and (3) the *Exemplar Series*. The aim of the *Exemplar Series* is the same as that of *Standards for the English Language Arts* (NCTE/IRA, 1996): "to ensure that all students develop the literacy skills they need to succeed in school and in various areas of life" (p. 68). The exemplars and portfolios in this book are intended to make visible to all stakeholders in the educational process the kinds of tasks teachers of English language arts value, the levels of performance that frequently co-exist in a single classroom, and the criteria by which student performances are often evaluated.

It is unfortunate, but true, that many teachers of English language arts still carry on their work in isolation from a professional community and rarely see work by students other than their own. Likewise, many students in English language arts classrooms lack opportunities to study and discuss the work of other students in other classrooms and to evaluate their own performance with reference to standards and/or rubrics. The intent of this book is to put the exemplars and portfolios into the hands of those who stand to benefit most from them—teachers and students.

Three final caveats are in order. (1) Use this book to develop your own local assessment, not as a substitute for it; (2) Use this book as a resource to develop your own course outline, not as *the* course outline; and (3) Use this book to develop your own exemplars, rubrics, and commentaries. Teachers at the local level need to work together to determine how they rank student work.

This book is only a bare sketch of what there is to know about the performance levels of students on the NCTE/IRA standards. The value of this book will be in the processes it generates and the discussions it inspires about what we, the English language arts teaching profession, K–12, value in student work.

Editors

Miles Myers received his B.A. in rhetoric, his M.A. in English, his M.A.T. in English and Education, and his Ph.D. (Language and Learning Division) at the University of California–Berkeley. He has served as the Executive Director of the National Council of Teachers of English since 1990, and has been president of the Central California Council of Teachers of English (in the 1960s), a vice president of the California Association of Teachers of English (in the 1970s), president of the Oakland Federation of Teachers-AFT (in the 1960s), and president of the California Federation of Teachers-AFT (in the 1980s). He was a co-director and the administrative director of the Bay Area, California, and National Writing Projects during the first ten years of their development (1975–1985), and for almost thirty years, he has been secretary-treasurer and later president of Alpha Plus Corporation, a nonprofit corporation of preschools in Oakland, California. He taught high school English for many years, primarily at Oakland High School, where he was department chair until 1975, when he left for the University of California–Berkeley. He served as Co-director and Administrative Director of the Bay Area, California, and National Writing Projects (1975–1985). He taught English methods courses at the University of California–Berkeley for five years, at the University of Illinois Urbana-Champaign for three years, and at various other institutions for shorter periods of time. He was co-director of the literacy unit of New Standards, and he has served on the advisory boards of the Center for the Study of Writing at the University of California–Berkeley, the National Research Center on Literature Teaching and Learning at the State University of New York at Albany, and the Board on Testing and Assessment of the National Academy of Science. He has received the Distinguished Service Award from the California Association of Teachers of English, the Ben Rust Award for Service from the California Federation of Teachers-AFT, and an Exemplary Service Award from the California Council of Classified Employees. He has authored six books and monographs as well as many articles on the teaching of English.

Elizabeth Spalding received her B.A. in Latin and English and M.A. in Latin from West Virginia University, and her Ph.D. in Curriculum Studies and Language Education from Indiana University-Bloomington. She is assistant professor in the Department of Curriculum and Instruction at the University of Kentucky. Previously, she was Project Manager for Standards at the National Council of Teachers of English, where she worked on the NCTE/IRA project to develop K–12 content standards and managed the New Standards project to develop performance assessment tasks and a portfolio assessment system. She has conducted numerous workshops on portfolio scoring and other assessments. She taught high school English, French, and Latin for many years in West Virginia and in the Department of Defense Dependents Schools–Pacific Region. Her research interests include teacher perspectives, teacher education, and alternative assessment of literacy. She has authored several articles on alternative assessment and the experiences of novice teachers.

Exemplar — Early

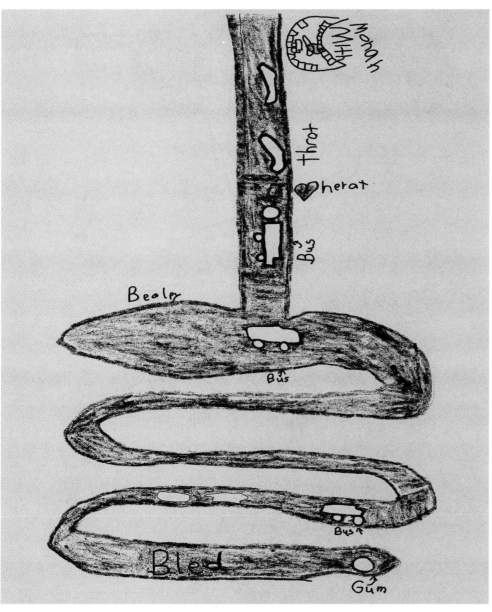

R u b r i c

Cognition: Fluent use of visual line and printed letters.

Rhetoric: A title and a code list would have helped the audience. The code list (bus, heart, teeth), with definitions, would have helped the audience understand the meaning quickly.

Conventions: The graphic conventions here are not as informative as those used in the face/body graphic (fluent). Where is the body?

Ideas: The student has some grasp of the basic ideas about the digestive system. A title ("The Digestive Tract") would have helped. The bus and heart logo are excellent.

Commentary

This representation is close to fluent. In this sample, the students focused on the digestive system itself. Thus, it is not clear whether the audience will understand its relationship to the body as a whole. At the top, the students show the Magic School Bus entering the mouth ("monah," "mith"). The teeth and epiglottis may be seen. The students show the journey of food (and the bus) down the throat past the heart ("herat"). The bus enters the belly ("Bealey") and continues its journey through the intestines, which are not labeled but are clearly represented. Evidently, the bus will end its journey in a large wad of gum. The students used bright red crayon to show the circulation of blood ("Bled"). Although the written language is simple, it is effectively combined with visual language. Spelling problems need to be corrected. The spelling of mouth contributes to serious confusions. As a whole, the drawing shows that the students have a good understanding of the purpose and organization of the digestive system. This effort is quite good.

Exemplar

Rubric

Cognition: The visual lines and the uses of print are fluent.

Conventions: The students make excellent use of graphic conventions and the writing, although clear, has many spelling problems.

Commentary

The students have situated the digestive system inside a human body. The placement of the parts is reasonably accurate. The parts are drawn in correct relationship (scale) to one another. Caption sentences clearly explain the function of each part: (translations) "Your teeth help you cut up your food in little pieces." "Your [esophageal] tube lets food get down." "Your throat holds food." "You have to let your food digest." "This is your exit tube." The students skillfully combine written and visual language to accomplish the task.

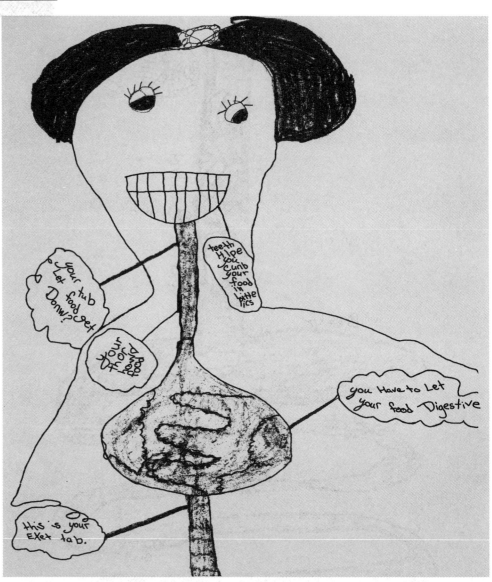

Connections to Standards

	STANDARDS											
Targeted	1	2	3	4	5	6	7	8	9	10	11	12
Supplementary	1	2	3	4	5	6	7	8	9	10	11	12

The targeted standards are 4, 5, and 6. These students have used visual representation as a strategy to convey their interpretation of a text (6). The students have also adjusted their written and visual language to communicate with an audience of peers (4). Visual representations, such as concept maps, Venn diagrams, and illustrations can play an important role in the development of a piece of writing (5). Visual representations, such as charts, graphs, and multimedia presentations, can also serve as vehicles for creating and communicating knowledge. The secondary standards are 10 and 12. Students whose first language is not English can use visual representation and their first language to develop competency in English language arts (10). Students can use visual representation to accomplish their own purposes (12), such as designing brochures and enhancing oral presentations.

T a s k

Expressive writing includes journals, diaries, and sometimes compositions intended to be read by others. For assessment purposes in this project, expressive writing involves observations, thoughts, or reflections. It may describe a scene or explore the significance of a person, object, or memory. It always has some focus around which the expressive details cluster. These pieces are usually descriptive, reflective, or exploratory. They may be informative in the sense that the writer conveys some specific information about a subject or event. They often incorporate the narrative strategies of autobiography or story. Expressive writing provides a foundation and is often the precursor for other, more formal kinds of writing. Expressive writing requires emotional and/or personal engagement on the part of the author, engagement which is communicated to the reader, but expressive writing does not adhere to the strict requirements of narrative, description, argument, and comparison/contrast. It is more important developmentally for fourth-grade students because it allows young writers to use writing as a way to develop fluency, to discover and clarify what they think, and to grow in their ability to perceive and reflect. The task presented here asked students to respond to the following line: *"This is what I see, think, and remember about . . ."*

Exemplar — High

R u b r i c

Cognition: The writer demonstrates fluency in expressing ideas, observations, and memories. The writing flows naturally without a code breakdown.

Rhetoric: The writer uses lively, concrete, and sometimes sophisticated language. The writing is conversational and natural, often revealing an individual and authentic voice. There are only minor lapses or inconsistencies in the focus.

Linguistics/Conventions: The top papers are almost completely free of missteps in structure and conventions.

Themes/Ideas: The writer explores ideas and may take risks to shape ideas. The writing demonstrates insightful and reflective thinking. The writer may explore an event or experience using relevant details and ideas.

> What a discovery I made!!!! About two years ago I discovered hockey. It was when my dad was watching a hockey game because when he was at a Flyers game when the Flyers won the Stanley Cup. I came over to him and said, "What are you watching, Daddy?" So he said he was watching a hockey game. I sat down and watched the game and I thought it was great. My family went to two Kings playoff games. I got to meet a few of the players. My favorite players are Wayne Gretzky and Jari Kurri. I think hockey is the best sport ever made. At school I always talk about hockey. The night I always will remember is the time I got a Wayne Gretzky game-used stick. I remember we were sitting down front and he glanced

Paper continued on page 34

Commentary

In this commendable performance, the writer demonstrates facility in expressing ideas, observations, and feelings. The writer clearly maintains focus on the importance of discovering hockey, from the first sentence to the last. The use of exclamation marks at the end of the opening sentence works quite well for this sample. Exclamation marks could probably not work in other forms. The sample is nearly error-free. The transition from the discovery (watching TV at Dad's house) to the game-stick episode is awkward, three or four (Kings playoff, players, great game…) potential ideas are introduced and dropped at this point. Nevertheless, the organization works. The scramble of ideas at this point is part of the expressive excitement. The concluding sentence brings us full circle, back to the opening sentence.

at me every so often. After the game he had brought his sticks out and he said, "I have a stick for you buddy" I was so happy I kept thanking him over and over. I play hockey right now. I play center and I also play street hockey. I have won three trophies and two medals. I was in a Wayne Gretzky article when he came back from an injury. Everybody knows about me loving hockey. That discovery was very important to me.

One day in 1992 I found a remote control truck I wanted to know how it worked. So I asked my dad if I could use some of his tools he said "OK" And I went to work taking the truck apart. When I was done I saw it worked by micro chips, wires lots of diffrent things that were very interesting It made me feel so happy and amazed I showed it to my dad. he was very proud of me And it was a wonderful feeling. I also learned something I learned you can make many diffrent discoveries if you put your mind and time to it.

Commentary

In this paper the writer clearly addresses what she sets out to do: "to know how it [remote control truck] worked." The writing is clear and flows smoothly; however, the writer develops ideas in a somewhat predictable manner, with more telling than showing. The writing shows some evidence of reflective thinking when the writer concludes with "I learned you can make many different discoveries if you put your mind and time to it." In general, the writing shows interesting thinking but lacks the insightful and exploratory quality of that found in higher papers.

Exemplar

Middle

R u b r i c

Cognition: The writing, although coherent, lacks the ease and fluency shown by writers of high papers.

Rhetoric: The writer reveals an individual voice, but does not always connect clearly with an audience. For example, in this sample, the writer introduces the "remote truck" without any background about what a "remote truck" is. Later "truck" becomes "trick" and the audience is confused again.

Linguistics/Conventions: The writing is clear with predictable sentences and word choice. "And" and "so" are frequent sentence transitions, suggesting an early episodic development in organization. The incident is well-told and has some overall coherence. The writer displays limited use of strategies.

Themes/Ideas: The writer develops ideas in a somewhat predictable fashion but show some engagement in exploring thoughts. The writing may reveal flashes of interesting thinking or a vivid impression, but ideas develop less fully. The writing may show some evidence of thoughtful attention to the requirements of the prompt. But these writers may either use details that overbalance the ideas or may be sparse in the use of details. Characters and/or events are presented clearly, and are relevant to the forms of a paper.

Exemplar

R u b r i c

Cognition: The writer demonstrates less fluency than is characteristic of the higher papers. The writing may ramble or rely on listing as a cognitive strategy.

Rhetoric: The paper is written in a flat, uninvolved voice. The writing shows some lack of control in handling word choice.

Linguistics/Conventions: The control of language structure and conventions leaves much to be desired. The overall text structure is often list-like, in this paper sometimes taking the form of one "I got" after another.

Themes/Ideas: Writers explore few ideas and thoughts and usually show little engagement. The writing rarely shows evidence of thinking that goes beyond a statement of ideas or a list of events. For example, in this paper we find "It was, It was, I got, I got, I got, sister got, mom got," and so on. Writers may place an action or event in a vague context; readers may be unsure about either the time or the place. Some details may be irrelevant.

I found Gold at my grandmas pond in Angels camp. I felt happy Because It was five pounds. It was vary fun because I got to spend it all. I got a New Bike. I got a Terbo hamer. I got what ever I wan't. My sister got what ever she wanted. My mom got what ever she wanted. My dad got wharever ne wtanred. My sister got a new Bike and new close and new shows. I got new shows and close. I got a Trail TO. My grandmas pound is dep t has fish and grass in it. My grand mas pond is in Angels camp.

Commentary

The choppy writing reflects the writer's focus on sentence-level composition. The sentences are generally understandable, but the absence of transitions makes the text confusing and sometimes tedious. The tedious repetition of "I got" is interrupted with apparently irrelevant details. For example, why are we told the depth of the pond (spelled "Pound" at one point)? Poor spelling, missing word connections ("what ever"), and other problems continue to harm the text.

Connections to Standards

	STANDARDS											
	1	2	3	4	5	6	7	8	9	10	11	12
Targeted	1	2	3	4	5	6	7	8	9	10	11	12
Supplementary	1	2	3	4	5	6	7	8	9	10	11	12

An expressive writing prompt targets writing standards 4, 5, and 6. When embedded in classroom instruction, it may take many forms. For example, expressive writing might be used to respond to a wide range of literature and nonliterary texts (1, 2) or as part of a research project (7). Because expressive writing encourages students to discover, explore, and clarify ideas, it can help students develop an understanding of and respect for diversity (9). Students whose first language is not English might use their first language while composing (e.g., choosing to use words in the first language) (10). Students can use expressive writing to accomplish their own purposes, such as keeping a journal or diary or contributing to a class book of memoirs (11, 12).

Task

In this task, students were asked to write a description or narrative about something or someone from their direct personal experience. The following selections come from a fourth-grade class. Students revised, edited, and word-processed these papers before including them in their writing portfolios.

Exemplar High

My Trip to Disney World

A long time ago when I was six years old, my granny and Aunt Anna had planned to go to Disney World. The big day finally arrived. I woke up, took a both, and put on some clothes. My granny packed my suitcase because I was to small of course. I was so excited about going to Disney World. We put all of our stuff in the back of the car and left.

Next we came to my Aunt's house. My cousin and I hopped in the back of the car. My aunt put her stuff in the back of the car, hopped in the car, and left home.

After a while when we were out of the city I got hungry. I asked my granny could I have something to drink and eat. She looked in the cooler and got us a grape pop and some Cheese-It's. We were so hungry that we almost ate the whole box.

The next thing I knew, I was looking at these tall buildings. We had been in the car for almost ten and a half hours. I asked my granny, "Where were we?" and she said "Florida." I was so happy we were in Florida that I started shouting.

After I stopped shouting we looked for a hotel. We found one with a big indoor swimming pool. My cousin and I got to go swimming. After that we had to get our hair done because our hair had chlorine in it. For dinner, we ate chicken salad, chicken, hot wings, potatoe salad, chips, dip, pimiento cheese and crackers.

We went to bed that night dreaming about Disney World. The next morning I woke up excited, ready for the fun day to begin. I took a bath and my granny brought us some Mickey and Minnie outfits to wear. We packed our bags because we were going to Disney World to stay a while. We put our stuff in my granny's car, and stopped by the office at the hotel, and gave them a key.

Finally we were to Disney World. I had butterflies in my tummy because I was so exciited.

When we got there the line was so long but I did not care, I was so exciited. I did not know what to do. It was finally our turn in line. We got on some rides and we went in the Haunted House, it was scary. We took a lot of pictures. It began to rain, so my granny went into a shop and got us some raincoats. I met Goofy, Minnie, and Mickey. My granny took my picture with the characters. I had a juice and some cotton candy. It was time for the exciting day to end.

On the way home, I was so tired that I feel asleep. My granny had to carry me in the house. That is a day I will never forget, especially when I was six going on seven.

Rubric

Cognition: The writer, who knows how to elaborate about episodes, shows excellent observation of details. The writer is also fluent and is rarely hindered by encoding problems.

Rhetoric: The writer has an excellent understanding of audience relationships, orienting the reader to the time of the story and foreshadowing for the reader the unfolding plot. In this sample, the writer establishes for the audience anticipation of excitement ("The big day," "was so excited . . . ," "I was so happy we were in Florida . . . ," "dreaming about Disney World").

Linguistics/Conventions: The writer has an excellent grasp of text structure. In this case, at the opening and closing, the student establishes the time frame of the story, giving the reader the perspective of a distant past. The paragraphing of the writer segments the important time periods of the story. The writer's grammatical practices are excellent, but there may be a few lapses.

Commentary

This writer charms us from the beginning ("a long time ago when I was six years old"); soon, we are on our way to Florida. The travelers are out of their home city in one paragraph and in Florida in the next. The writer keeps us anticipating Disney World with shouts, claims ("I was so excited"), and finally "butterflies in my tummy." Along the way the writer gives us the interesting details about food, concluding with juice and cotton candy at Disney World. The writing flows easily, but there are a few lapses in spelling ("both" for bath, "to" for too) and punctuation. The writer closes with the uncertain but charming, "a day I will never forget, especially when I was six going on seven." The writer has come full circle, repeating the time frame at the beginning. This sample shows an excellent grade 4–5 writer.

Exemplar

Rubric

Cognition: The writer is able to organize descriptions around episodes, but does not elaborate these episodes. The writer does not have serious encoding problems.

Rhetoric: The writer is somewhat uncertain about distance to audience, but does have good control of distance to personal subjects. The writer often fails to engage the audience with a sharp image or dramatic event. Some figures of speech help enliven the work of the writer, but the absence of elaboration keeps the description too general.

Linguistics/Conventions: The writer reveals a good grammatical sense in the writing, but there are lapses in conventions here and there. The writer's understanding of text structure is adequate for the task. Frequent, thin paragraphs, are often typical of the middle writer.

Mamaw and I

Has there been a recent death in your family? My Mamaw died at three sixteen in the morning. She meant alot to me. When she died, I felt like fine china breaking. But I was happy for her because she is gone to a better place but still sad because she is gone away from me.

One fun thing I liked to do with her was go to breakfast. She would come to my house and take me to breakfast at Hardees. Sometimes we made homemade breakfast. Most of the time when we did that, we made fried country ham with scrambled eggs.

After breakfast we'd go to the park and slide down the slide. My favorite thing at the park was burying one another in the sand. Sometimes Mawmaw buried herself. When I would be walking, she'd jump up and scare me!

Sometimes I'd spend the night at her house and help teach the pet bird to talk. We taught him to whistle when someone whistled to him. Also when she had a baby guinea pig, we helped feed the baby with a bottle.

Most weekends we spent together she took me to the mountains. sometimes we could get souvenirs. Other times we would just look at different styles of cloths and shoes.

I hope you keep good memories. I'll always remember my Mamaw. It makes me feel better when I remember the good times Mamaw and I had together.

Commentary

This writer begins the description with an awkward question to the reader ("Has there been a recent death in your family?"). Without any transition, the writer begins with Mamaw's death. The writer is trying to build a bridge between the personal experiences of the reader and the writer, but the bridge is awkward. The same problem returns at the end when the writer addresses the reader, "I hope you keep good memories" and then abruptly shifts to the writer's memories.

The writer has some good moments, for example, "When she died, I felt like fine china breaking" and the closing line. But the absence of elaboration weakens the writing. For example, we needed to know more about those mountain trips in the next to last paragraph. What mountains? How far away? Souvenirs, clothes, and shoes—are these details the only matter worth reporting? Something important seems to be missing. Nevertheless, this writer has written an adequate description.

Exemplar Low

The Good and Bad Life

I was going to football practice. My mom was taking me. We were on our way and the light was red. My mom was not paying attention. She ran the red light and a car was coming. I yelled we are going to get hit! BOOM! It hit the side of my mom's car. It put a dent in it. But we were not hurt.

Next the cops came. My mom's car would not start. I was scared. My mom had to call my dad. So he could take us home. When I saw my dad I was not scared anymore.

A truck came and took our car to be fixed. I said thanks to the man. My mom checked the car. It was a little better, but they couldn't fix the dent. At least we were all okay!

R u b r i c

Cognition: The primary cognitive strategy is a chain or list of details or episodes.

Rhetoric: The writer does not attempt to establish a rhetorical relationship with the audience. Low papers often start in the middle of an exposition, leaving out thesis sentences, overall direction, and other indicators to the audience.

Linguistics/Conventions: Low papers have serious problems in text or language.

Themes/Ideas: The ideas are not clearly identified and elaborated in low papers.

Commentary

This low paper suffers from a choppy, unelaborated structure at both the sentence and text level. There are not too many significant problems in basic conventions, but there are a few minor lapses. The paper, which has no introductory sentence, needs one. The title is too vague to be much help. Many necessary details are left out of the story (How long ago did it happen? Tell us more about the dent. What did Dad say when he arrived? Was the truck an auto-puller? What did the police say? Why was the car better?). The task asks for a description, and the student writes something closer to a telegram.

Connections to Standards

	STANDARDS											
Targeted	1	2	3	4	5	6	7	8	9	10	11	12
Supplementary	1	2	3	4	5	6	7	8	9	10	11	12

The targeted standards assessed in the task are 4, 5, and 6. Writing descriptions of personal experience requires students to adjust their use of written language to communicate effectively to a particular audience (4). Students use a wide range of strategies and various writing process elements to produce finished pieces (5). Students apply their knowledge of language structure, conventions, and genre to create descriptions of personal experience (6). Other standards possibly assessed by this task are 1, 2, 9, 10, 11, and 12. As part of ongoing classroom instruction, students might read and respond to a variety of memoirs, biographies, and autobiographies (1, 2, 7). Reading and responding to such texts can help students develop an understanding of and respect for diversity (9). Students whose first language is not English might use their first language in composing descriptions of personal experience (e.g., writing dialogue in or choosing to use words in the first language) (10). Students can use this genre to accomplish their own purposes, such as exploring their own or their family's life histories (11, 12).

T a s k

The responses used in this section come from the 1992 writing assessment of the National Assessment of Educational Progress (NAEP), *Writing Report Card.* The 1992 writing assessment required fourth-grade students to write an informative description of a favorite story within a twenty-five minute time period. The Favorite Story Prompt allowed students to use a favorite story that they had read, heard, or seen at the movies. Students were encouraged to provide interesting details that would explain the appeal of the story.

To be effective, informative writing must convey knowledge and ideas with clarity and detail. In this kind of task, the subject matter being conveyed may be based on the writer's personal knowledge or experience, or it may involve the synthesis of new information presented to the writer. Whether the writing involves the familiar, the new, or a mixture of both, informative thought can require a wide range of analytic and evaluative skills, from writing a letter or filling out a job application to more complex professional or academic tasks requiring description, analysis, and explanation. The following general guidelines were used to evaluate the written responses to tasks of this kind. This task, in addition to assessing writing, is also assessing how well students comprehend what they read. This task does not assess interpretation or even analysis of reading, only comprehension. This does not mean that students do not interpret or analyze. Thus, the scores used here (not the NAEP score) are intended to suggest that the student did or did not understand the story. A report of information which is clearly inaccurate does not receive a high score. For this informative task, scorers focused particularly on quality of description (clarity and use of detail). In the NAEP scoring, papers were scored according to the following six-point scale, which has been collapsed into high, middle, and low in this book:

Scale in This Book	NAEP Scale
High: Samples of high papers in this task come from NAEP samples titled "Extensively elaborated" and "Elaborated"	**6 Extensively elaborated.** In these papers, students create a well-developed, detailed, and well-written response to the task. They show a high degree of control over the various elements of writing. These responses may be similar to "5" responses, but they are better organized, more clearly written, and less flawed. **5 Elaborated.** In these papers, students write a well-developed and detailed response to the task. They may go beyond the requirements of the task.
Middle: Samples of middle papers in this task are from "Developed" category	**4 Developed.** In these papers, students provide a response to the task that contains necessary elements. However, these papers may be unevenly developed.
Low: Low samples come from the bottom categories of the NAEP scale	**3 Minimally developed.** In these papers, students provide a response to the task that is brief, vague, or somewhat confusing. **2 Undeveloped response to task.** In these papers, students begin to respond to the task, but they do so in a very abbreviated, confusing, or disjointed manner. **1 Response to topic.** In these papers, students respond to some aspect of the topic but do not appear to have fully understood the task. Or, they recopy text from the prompt.

Hicory

Exemplar **High**

"In a land far away there was a lot of animals starving, except the rabbit. Well there was a rabbit named Hicory. Now Hicory was very sligh. He could talk anybody into anything. Well Hicory was looking for some food. So Hicory decided to play a trick on the Hens for his dinner. So he got a bucket of water a broom a cage and a violin. He went down to an old farm and started to play the violin. the hens came out and started to dance. After awhile Hicory stopped playing and the hens asked, "Why did you come to play for us," and rabbit said "To cheer you up", and the hen said " you are so nice" and the hen asked "why do you have that bucket of water" "because " I know you get thirsty dancing" said Hicory then the hen asked "why do you have that cage." then Hicory said "to run in if it rains." "oh your so nice" said the hen. Suddenly Hicory put the broom in the water, stuck it in the air and shook it all around he called "It's Raining " all the hens ran in the cage Hicory closed the door. Hicory had a very good dinner.

R u b r i c

Cognition: The writer has code fluency.

Rhetoric: In both the introduction and conclusion, the writer has a good sense of rhetorical distance.

Linguistics/Conventions: The text structure depends too often on "and," "so," and "well" for sentence transitions. Nevertheless, the paper is well organized and flows smoothly. The writer shows an excellent command of quotation marks. Run-on sentences, subject-verb agreement problems, comma errors— these are a few of the problems keeping this paper from being at the highest level of high papers. It was rated a low high paper. Remember these papers are written in a twenty-five-minute period.

Themes/Ideas: The paper captures quite well the ideas and themes of the story. The detailed elaboration is impressive.

Commentary

Some high papers may have some convention problems which do not interfere with meaning. Very few fourth graders (2 percent) wrote extensively elaborated papers, providing complete and relevant details about the setting, characters, episodes, and ending.

Exemplar

Rubric

Cognition: The writer has code fluency.

Rhetoric: The introduction is barely adequate.

Text/Linguistics/Conventions: Commas and run-on sentences are problems throughout many middle papers. Nevertheless, these papers are easy to read and understand. Though text structure is often list-like and too choppy, the organization is clear.

Themes/Ideas: The student has a good grasp of the ideas in the story. The ideas in the middle papers are often simple.

It all begain in the 1863. There were a boy named Tim how was a wood cuter he loved to cut woods that was its job back in 1863. One day Tim went out to cut some woods. He cut the frist one and went to the other one. When he was done with all the cuting, he was very tierd so he said I.ll go home and rest and then I.ll come back. When He went back home & he saw that his house was birnd, So he said thats ok I.ll just get all those woods that I cut down and make a new house for me, He was all done making the house, so he went in and lived happly ever after.

Commentary

This paper provided a clear and comprehensive summary of the story. Nearly one-quarter of the fourth graders (22 percent) wrote responses rated as "developed." Although the summaries contained enough information to be considered developed, they lacked elaboration. In this example, the student has provided a complete, albeit brief, summary of how Tim the Woodcutter rebuilds his home.

Exemplar Low

> Donny Campoin of the World
> Once there was a boy named Donny
> whene he was born his mother
> died. And it was only him and his dad.
> Once his dad told him his deep dark
> secret and it was: Me and your mom
> Yous ea to go out hunting. So wonce
> his dad went out hunting and Donny
> woke up and went out to there shak
> and got a Baby ostin and he drove
> to the wood and go this dad out of
> the hole.

R u b r i c

Cognition: The writer lacks some fluency with the code.

Rhetoric: The writer captures some of the rhetorical distance of the original story. Title and introduction provide a helpful frame for the story.

Linguistics/Conventions: Too many problems produce a paper which is often almost unreadable.

Commentary

At the low levels, minimally developed responses may provide a summary of the story, but leave major gaps. Often these gaps resulted from the student failing to provide an adequate overview of the story's theme or plot line, or omitting a crucial story element, such as the ending. In the NAEP scoring, nearly half of the fourth-graders' responses (45 percent) fell into the score category given to this sample. In this example, the response is so vague that it is difficult for a reader to understand the plot. The frequent errors make the papers in the low category nearly unreadable in parts.

Connections to Standards

	STANDARDS											
Targeted	1	2	3	///4///	///5///	///6///	7	8	9	10	11	12
Supplementary	///1///	///2///	///3///	///4///	///5///	///6///	///7///	///8///	///9///	10	11	///12///

Reports of information are targeted to writing standards 4, 5, and 6. Supplementary standards which might be assessed include 1, 2, 3, 7, 8, 9, and 12. Reports of information might require students to read and respond to a wide range of literary and nonliterary texts (1, 2) and to apply to a wide range of strategies as they interpret and evaluate these texts (3). Students might also conduct research (7) and use a variety of resources to gather and synthesize information and to create and communicate knowledge (8). Depending on the topic and focus, reports of information can help students develop an understanding of and respect for diversity (9) and to use language to accomplish their own purposes (12), e.g., enjoyment or the exchange of information.

T a s k

Students were asked to submit (1) a plan for an argument written as a letter and (2) the final draft of the letter-argument. The plan was to be organized around five questions or columns about a purpose (the argument): who (audience), what (subject), why (reasons for purpose or argument), possible objections from the other side(s), and possible alternative arguments to counter the possible objections. The plan and the argument were scored together as high, middle, or low. This task and these samples come from a multistate project of the Council of Chief State School Officers.

Exemplar High

The Plan:

Purpose: To have no homework for the rest of the year.

Who (Audience)	What (Subject)	Why (Reasons)	Possible Objections	Possible Arguments
Mrs. _____	No Homework	• It's to nice outside to be stuck inside doing homework. • We have sports and other activity's at night and in the afternoon that don't give us a chance to do homework. • We'll have a lot of homework next year so why not give us a break for the rest of this year.	• It's not the end of the year yet. you still need to learn. • Doing homework for the rest of the year will help you get ready for next year at Redding. • You have all summer to play so just wait until then.	• I think that we learn and cover enough in school that we don't need homework. • We have done enough in school that has at least got me ready for Redding. Plus after school. Instead of homework we could be doing things that we wouldn't have a choice to do in Redding like playing outside and doing sports. • But people might be doing something that won't allow them to get outside and play.

The Letter-Argument:

Dear Mrs.

Could you please think about not giving us anymore homework for the rest of the year? I ask this because it's too nice outside to be stuck inside doing loads of homework. Besides some of us have sports and other activities in the afternoon which doesn't give us a chance to do our homework. But in some cases sports let us learn too; so it wouldn't be like we would stop thinking. Also, we'll have ton's of homework next year, so why not give us the rest of the year off.

I know you might say that the year's not over and we still need to learn and homework will get us ready for next year at but I think we have learned and covered enough already. I also know that we will still continue having work which will sharpen our skills.

I think you also might say that we have all summer to play, but some people might be doing something that won't allow them to get out.

Please just think about it.

Sincerely, _____

P.S. You don't really like correcting homework do you?

Rubric

Cognition: The writer has code fluency.

Rhetoric: The writer has a good audience relationship. The weakness is the selection of ideas to support the argument.

Linguistics/Conventions: There are some problems but they are not confusing meaning.

Themes/Ideas: The ideas are adequate but hardly inspiring or deeply persuasive.

Commentary

The paper is well-written, but the ideas are weak. A strong argument would look for reasons the other side would find persuasive. This writer uses only reasons appealing to him/her (sports). This is a good effort, but it is a weak high paper. The problems are frequent but not disruptive. Missing *-ed* (tense problem), commas missing, reference problem ("which"), misuse of apostrophe ("ton's"), spelling, run-on—these are a few of the convention errors and structural problems in the paper. The author does try to state the view of the opposition ("you might say"), and at the end the author states the appeal to the reader as a question ("P.S. You don't really . . . do you?"). The overall effectiveness is quite good in many ways. The evidence does present different kinds of support for the argument.

Exemplar — Middle

The Plan:

Purpose: To convince my Mom & Dad to let me try out for the football team.

Who (Audience)	What (Subject)	Why (Reasons)	Possible Objections Mom Dad	Possible Arguments Me
Mom & Dad	To convince Mom & Dad to let me try out for the football team	• I like to play football • I love to run, and you run a lot in football • I know all the rules so I will play fair.	• You might get hurt. • I'll have to drive you to all your games and practices • It costs to much money • You probably won't play much • The coaches are strict • You might not even make the team.	• We wear pads and helmets • Maybe Mom Mom can drive me to practices. • I'll pay half • I going to work hard so he will play me • So are my soccer coaches • I'm going to try my hardist

The Letter-Argument:

Dear Mom & Dad,
    I know you said no about trying out for the football team but I've been practicing a lot. I love football.
    I know its a lot of money to try out but I've been saving my allowance. I understand that transportatin is a problem but I can ask Mom Mom or Pop Pop to take me to some practices I know youre afraid that I'll get hurt but we wear pads and helmets. The coaches are strict but I'm used to it because my soccer coaches are strict too. I know you think I won't play much because I'm small, but every thing I do I'm good at.
    Can you please think about it for a while? Thanks.
                          Your Son.

Rubric

Cognition: A fluent writer.

Rhetoric: The writer establishes some good connections with audience. The closing question reestablishes the audience relationship. But the writer is not able to take the point of view of a different person.

Linguistics/Conventions: Barely adequate. Commas, periods, apostrophes, spelling, and many other problem areas seriously weaken the paper. These errors make reading the paper very difficult.

Themes/Ideas: The ideas supporting the argument are barely adequate.

Commentary

This paper is barely adequate. The argument makes almost no appeal to the needs and concerns of the parents. One exception is the detailed response to parental concerns about being hurt. The "small" argument at the end, however, tends to undermine the good reasons why parents should not worry about the son being hurt. Another exception is the student's suggestion that the student will pay ("saving my allowance"). But the student does not develop the idea and announce explicitly, "I will pay!" The solution presented for transportation is "Mom Mom or Pop Pop" (grandparents, presumably). This solution is not persuasive to parents. The plan shows clearly why the writer is not persuasive. The writer thinks "I like to play," "I love to run," and "I am going to try my hardest" are persuasive to another person. None of these reasons answer the charge that the student will be hurt.

Exemplar Low

The Plan:

Purpose: To persuaide parents on going to the mall

Who (Audience)	What (Subject)	Why (Reasons)	Possible Objections	Possible Arguments
parents	Persuading parents on going to the mall.	• Haven't been there in a while • need new clothes or shoes • everybody might need or want something • could pay for it with our money	• But can't go the next night • can always get new clothes or shoes • you can always get what you want or need some place else • cost a lot	• But there is a sale on anything and today is the last day • They might not have the right size • But no other place sells what you want and it's a limited time only • found out it doesn't cost too much

The Letter-Argument:

Dear Mom,   May 19, 1996

Could we please go to the mall? We havn't been there for a long time I understand you havn't felt. like going to mall lately but you said that you felt better. Anyway I need new clothes and shoes because I have just about out grown my shoes. and I'm starting to out grow my clothes too. I really do need them. I understand that you think I really don't need new shoes because it don't look as if I need them but I really do. Besides I heard you and dad both want something from the mall. Anyway I could pay for the clothes and shoes with my own mony. Again I understand that think it will cost a lot of mony. but I found out that clothes and shoes are on sale. Come on mom. I promise i'll do all of my chores and get all my homework done early. Please?
                                    Sincerely,

Rubric

Cognition: Fluent writer.

Rhetoric: The "we" engages the audience in the project, and audience awareness is strong throughout.

Linguistics/Conventions: There are serious errors of structure and conventions.

Themes/Ideas: The ideas are a strong appeal to parents.

Commentary

Run-on sentences, capitalization, spelling problems, misplaced periods, missing words and commas, subject-verb agreement problems are among the numerous errors of structure and conventions in this paper. These missteps undermine what could have been an excellent argument. In fact, the content is stronger than that found in the middle paper. But the writing suffers from a serious absence of knowledge about conventions and linguistic structures. The final line is an appealing conclusion. The focus on the need for clothes and the fact that the writer will pay are both solid reasons for going to the mall.

Connections to Standards

	STANDARDS											
Targeted	1	2	3	4	5	6	7	8	9	10	11	12
Supplementary	1	2	3	4	5	6	7	8	9	10	11	12

The targeted standards are 4, 5, and 6. In writing arguments, students adjust their use of written language to communicate effectively with authentic audiences (4). The letters here show students using various strategies as they compose (i.e., completing an organizing framework) (5). The students have applied knowledge of language structure, conventions, and genre to create print texts (6). The supplementary standards are 1, 7, 8, and 12. As students grow more sophisticated in this genre (argument), they may read about problems and propose solutions (1), conduct research on issues (7), gather information from a variety of sources (8), and construct written arguments for various audiences. Students can use this genre to accomplish their own purposes (12), such as influencing school policy or speaking out on issues of national concern.

Introduction to Task and Rubric

There are four small tasks in this task. The responses used in this section were gathered from the 1992 survey of America's students by the National Assessment of Educational Progress (NAEP), *Reading Assessment Redesigned: Authentic Texts and Innovative Instruments in NAEP's 1992 Survey.* In this task, the 1992 assessment required fourth-grade students to reflect on and write about their understandings of one or more literary selections.

This task has two types of constructed response. The first type of constructed-response question is short, asking students to think and write briefly about their understandings. The second type (question 4) is an extended constructed-response question and is designed to prompt greater thought and reflection. In comparison to the multiple-choice questions that require students to select among an array of already developed responses, both types of constructed-response questions require students to generate their own ideas and to communicate them in writing.

In this assessment, students read and responded to *Amanda Clement: The Umpire in a Skirt,* an autobiographical essay about the first paid woman baseball umpire on record. Hired in 1904, she is now recognized in the Baseball Hall of Fame. The article describes how she learned the sport at an early age by being asked to umpire for her brother (Hank) and his friends, how well-accepted she became in her profession, and what she did in her later life. Amanda's story is set in the context that in 1904 women were not supposed to participate in professionalized sports like baseball. Ice skating and swimming were open to women.

The following NAEP rubric/framework was used to evaluate the reading responses. The NAEP rubric for literary responses focuses on accomplishment in initial understanding, development of an interpretation, personal reflection, and critical stance (see below). Responses to the short constructed-response questions (questions 1–3) were scored as either acceptable or unacceptable. Responses to the extended question (question 4) were scored on a four-point scale: extensive, essential, partial, or unsatisfactory. Three levels of response–high, middle, low–are presented here. These levels show degrees of accomplishment in various aspects of reading literacy as outlined in the rubric/framework. The four knowledge domains are represented in the framework below as follows: (1) the initial understanding is an indication of *cognitive fluency;* (2) the critical stance captures the reader's *rhetorical relationship* to the text; (3) interpretations capture the domain of *ideas and themes;* and (4) *linguistic conventions* are suggested throughout. The three ways of knowing are: (1) *Reading for Information* is *knowing that;* (2) *Reading to Perform a Task* is *knowing how;* and (3) *Reading for Literary Experience* is *knowing about,* at least for these assessment purposes.

In this task the next three questions are scored either high or low. The scale below was used to score responses to *Question Four only.* Parts of the rubric below are repeated in the rubrics for each question.

Scale in This Book	NAEP Scale	
High: High samples from NAEP's "Extensive" category	Level 4	**Extensive** Responses indicated that students had more fully considered the issues and, in doing so, had developed elaborated understandings and explanations.
Middle: Middle samples from NAEP's "Essential" level	Level 3	**Essential** Responses included enough detail and complexity to indicate that students had developed at least generally appropriate understandings of the passage and the question.
Low: Low samples from NAEP's "Partial" and "Unsatisfactory" level	Level 2	**Partial** Responses demonstrated some understanding, but it was incomplete, fragmented, or not supported with appropriate evidence or argument.
	Level 1	**Unsatisfactory** Responses reflected little or no understanding, or repeated disjointed or isolated bits from the passage.

The rubrics and commentaries are organized around the following reading framework:

NAEP's 1992 Reading Rubric/Framework
Constructing, Extending, and Examining Meaning

	Initial Understanding	Developing an Interpretation	Personal Reflection and Response	Demonstrating a Critical Stance
	Requires the reader to provide an initial impression or unreflected understanding of what was read.	Requires the reader to go beyond the initial impression to develop a more complete understanding of what was read.	Requires the reader to connect knowledge from the text with personal background knowledge. The focus here is on how the text relates to personal knowledge.	Requires the reader to stand apart from the text and consider it.
Reading for Literary Experience	What is the story/plot about? How would you describe the main character?	How did the plot develop? How did this character change from the beginning to the end of the story?	How did this character change your idea of _____? Is this story similar to or different from your own experiences?	Rewrite this story with ___ as a setting or ___ as a character. How does this author's use of ___ (irony, personification, humor) contribute to ___?
Reading for Information	What does this article tell you about _____? What does the author think about this topic?	What caused this event? In what ways are these ideas important to the topic or theme?	What current event does this remind you of? Does this description fit what you know about _____? Why or why not?	How useful would this article be for _____? Explain. What could be added to improve the author's argument?
Reading to Perform a Task	What is this supposed to help you do? What time can you get a nonstop flight to X?	What will be the result of this step in the directions? What must you do before this step?	In order to ___, what information would you need to find that you don't know right now? Describe a situation in which you could leave out step X.	Why is this information needed? What would happen if you omitted this?

T a s k   O n e:

Tell two ways in which Mandy's experience would be similar or different if she were a young girl wanting to take part in sports today.

An important reading skill is the ability to bring outside experiences and knowledge to an understanding of a text. The above short constructed-response question asked students to apply this ability to the Amanda Clement passage. Students' responses to short constructed-response questions were scored here according to a two-level rubric, such that a response was either acceptable or unacceptable. Responses scored as unacceptable (low) indicated little or no understanding of the passage and question. Responses scored as acceptable (high) indicated that the student had grasped both the passage and the question and was able to answer the question successfully.

High Exemplar

R u b r i c

Elaborated responses, including two ways arranged in coherent order.

Commentary

The example at left of an acceptable response indicates both an understanding of the obstacles Mandy confronted and an ability to tell whether those obstacles would be the same or different in the light of current circumstances. Acceptable responses focused on various ideas, such as how girls today are allowed to play sports, how baseball games today have more than one umpire, and how some sports are still inaccessible to women.

> Her experience would be diffrent today because girls are aloud to play sports. Her experience would be the the same in football because it is very rough

Low Exemplar

R u b r i c

Does not have two ways and the organization is disjointed. Serious language problems.

Commentary

Unacceptable responses reflected a lack of understanding of Mandy's experience, often invoking knowledge related to the text's topic, but in ways irrelevant to the text's concerns and the question's intent.

> she would have to no how to play sports I think she would still be good in base ball.

Task Two:

Give three examples showing that Mandy was not a quitter.

This short constructed-response question required fourth graders to collect evidence from a text to support an interpretation about a character or theme in the text, as in the following example.

Rubric

The three examples ("mother," "watch," and "kept going") are clearly presented.

One is her mother did not want her to umpire but she persuaded her mother to let her She did not quit when she had to watch and when she kept going.

Commentary

Acceptable responses indicated an understanding of how the passage presents Mandy's character, and an ability to choose specific information about Mandy from the passage that could be called upon to prove that she was not a quitter. Such responses usually referred to Mandy's determination to play, or to her career as a teacher and umpire, or both.

Rubric

The response does not answer the question.

she always was understanding.
she is cowaperitive
she hates to be mad alway happy.

Commentary

Unacceptable responses typically demonstrated a weak grasp of how Mandy is portrayed in the passage, and an inability to cite specific information.

Task Three:

What was Hank's role in Mandy's early career?

This relatively straightforward question about the relationship between characters and events was designed to measure students' global understanding of the text.

High Exemplar

Rubric

The response explains Hank's role and the results of his efforts.

Commentary

Acceptable responses demonstrated an understanding of how Hank assisted Mandy by letting her umpire.

Hank asked Mandy to unpire his game first. Then people saw how good she was they wanted her to unpire there games till mandy was famous.

Low Exemplar

Rubric

The response shows some minimal grasp of the story.

Commentary

Unacceptable responses may have showed some minimal grasp of events, but did not indicate an ability to relate events to one another or to characters. Some made reference to umpiring or to Hank, but without connecting either to the relationship between Hank's actions and Mandy's life.

Hank help her with her with baseball

T a s k   F o u r :

If she were alive today, what question would you like to ask Mandy about her career? Explain why the answer to your question would be important to know.

This extended question asked fourth graders to go beyond surface comprehension to demonstrate a fuller understanding of Amanda's career in light of her gender, times, personal experiences, or social experiences. Students were asked to provide evidence of such understanding by posing a relevant question not already answered in the passage, and by explaining the relevance of the question in terms of Mandy's life and times, or their own. Three levels of response are presented here: high, middle, and low.

R u b r i c

The question is clearly presented and the explanation for the question is very persuasive.

Exemplar **High**

Commentary

Responses reflecting extensive understanding demonstrated a richer understanding of the passage, indicating that the student has considered the more complex social or personal issues suggested by the passage. These responses, for example, might have contained questions about issues or feelings that emerge from consideration of the potential problems Mandy faced, placing her in a historical and social context. Very few students— 2 percent nationally—provided responses such as these.

I would ask if Mandy had a hard time with other people because she was a girl and participated in sports.

The answer would be important because I do not think it was fair that girls did not play sports like baseball hockey, basketball, and football a long time ago. Also it would be important because somebody else's answer would probably be different from Mandy's.

Exemplar

Middle

I would ask her why did she chose to be a good umpire and not a batter or somthing close to that tecnec. I would ask her that questoin because it is very important to me because, if she had bin a women batter. she might had gave women d chance to become more than an umpire. Women could be batters, and maybe play in the game.

Commentary

Middle responses demonstrated an overall understanding of Mandy's life and career. Some 31 percent of the national responses scored at this level. These responses contained at least one question specifically related to Mandy's career with a relevant explanation about the importance of that question.

R u b r i c

> A question may be presented, but the reasons are either disjointed or missing.

Exemplar — Low

How old are you? Can I have a picture of you.

Commentary

Unsatisfactory understanding was reflected in responses that demonstrated little or no understanding of Mandy's life or career. These students cited isolated or unrelated bits of information from the passage, or posed a question unrelated to Mandy's career or situation.

Connections to Standards

	STANDARDS											
	1	2	3	4	5	6	7	8	9	10	11	12
Targeted	▨	▨	▨	4	5	▨	7	8	9	10	11	12
Supplementary	▨	▨	▨	▨	5	▨	7	8	▨	▨	11	▨

Response to literary and informational texts requires students to apply a range of strategies to comprehend, interpret, evaluate, and critique texts (1, 2, 3, 6). These are the targeted standards. When embedded in classroom instruction, responses might include visual representations (4) and texts might also include such nonprint sources as films and television and radio broadcasts (1). Depending on the texts being read or viewed and the responses being elicited or offered, responses to literary and informational texts can help students develop an understanding of and respect for diversity (9). Students whose first language is not English can use their first language to develop understanding of texts (e.g., recording marginal notes, noting questions, translating key concepts into the first language) (10). Students can use responses to literary and informational texts to accomplish their own purposes, such as developing and exploring an interpretation of a self-selected novel or becoming informed on a political issue (12).

Task

The following reading task, taken from *A Sampler of English Language Arts Assessment: Elementary* from the California Department of Education, asks students to read a selection about the discovery of the painted caves of Lascaux, written by Jenny Wood. The student's score is determined by evaluating all the evidence of the performance, whether in the form of marginal notes, graphics, or extended written responses. The first step in this response was to write margin comments while reading. Responses from Student A are on the left and Students B and C on the right. How would you judge these comments?

Before you read: You are going to read a selection about the discovery of painted caves. Before you read, take a minute to think of what you already know about prehistoric cavemen.

As you read, you may mark up the selection in any way that helps you better understand or remember what you are reading.

My thoughts, feelings, and/or questions about what I'm reading.*

My thoughts, feelings, and/or questions about what I'm reading.*

My thoughts, feelings, and/or questions about what I'm reading.*

Excerpt from
An Amazing Discovery
by Jenny Wood

Student A
High Score

I think they should not go in because they do not have any supplies. I mean what if they fall and cannot get back up? They need rope and other stuff that will help them.

Do you mean they go to the same house for dinner? It looks like Simon is the smart one and Marcel is the spirited one.

It was a warm Sunday afternoon in September, 1940. Four friends, Marcel Ravidat, Jacques Marsal, Georges Agnel, and Simon Coencas, were exploring the woods on a hill overlooking the town of Montignac in southwest France.

Suddenly Marcel shouted to his friends.

"Come and look at this!"

Hearing the note of excitement in his voice, the three other boys ran to see what he had found. There between the roots of a dead tree was a dark, deep hole.

Jacques peered down into the darkness. "It looks as if it goes right down into the bowels of the earth."

The strange hole did seem to have no end. It was as if, down under the dead tree, there was a hollow bubble of dark nothingness.

"Perhaps it's the secret underground passage which leads to Lascaux Manor," said Georges. "You know, the one Monsieur Laval was telling us about at school."

"That would be a find!" said Simon. For years people had talked about this secret passage, but no one had ever found it.

"Come on then," urged Marcel. "What are we waiting for? Let's explore."

"No," said Simon, "not now. It'll be dark soon and there'll be trouble if we're not home for dinner. Let's do this properly. We should take a whole afternoon and we'll need a light and some ropes."

"You're right," said Jacques. "Why don't we come back on Thursday? We're

Student B
Middle Score

I feel exited on what will happen next and what they will do. I'm wondering if they will go down in the hole.

I would be scared and I don't think I would want to go down in because there might be something dangerous in it.

Student C
Low Score

Marcel shouted to his friends Come and look at this.

there was a dead tree. there was a hole under the tree.

*In the test for 1994, this wording has been changed to: My thoughts and/or questions about what I'm reading.

Student A
High Score

Marcel wants to do it so quickly that he doesn't think of what can happen to them until Simon reminds him.

That's a good idea. I wouldn't have thought of that myself.

I agree with Simon because I don't think they are professional explorers. Also, they should tell someone because what if they get trapped or killed before they get to tell about this amazing discovery? What if they die before they get famous for finding all of this?

---

off school that afternoon."

"OK then," agreed Marcel, although he didn't know how he would be able to wait four whole days.

But Thursday came soon enough. The boys met by the dead tree with a home-made oil lamp, a few bits of rope and a knife. They set to work clearing away the undergrowth from around the hole.

"How deep do you think it is?" asked Georges, peering down into the blackness.

"No idea," replied Simon. "Why don't we try throwing a few stones into it. We might be able to guess the depth by listening to the stones falling."

The stones fell and rolled for a long time.

"It must be very deep," said Simon. Perhaps we shouldn't go down."

"We'll just have to be careful," said Jacques. "Now come on, let's stop wasting time!"

One by one the boys squeezed through. They slid and tumbled down and down. At last they stopped, none the worse for the fall, at the bottom of the hole. Even the oil lamp had survived its journey.

In the lamp's dim light, the boys could see that they were in a huge underground chamber. The walls seemed to be covered with lines and dots.

"Turn up the lamp and hold it higher," said Georges. "I want to get a better look at these walls." His voice echoed through the cave.

Jacques did as he was asked. As the lamp began to light up the cave, the lines and spots seemed to grow into the shapes of bulls and deer. The walls were covered with paintings!

"These paintings must have been made by cavemen thousands of years ago."

"And no one has seen them for thousands of years!" added Simon.

It had taken them quite some time to get into the cave and already the light from the entrance was growing dim.

"We should really tell someone about this," said Simon.

"Not yet," Marcel replied decidedly. "I want to see it all before we let anyone else know. I think we should come back

---

Student B
Middle Score

I would want to go in again and see everything and keep it a secret and then go down and explore everything in the hole

---

Student C
Low Score

59

Student A
High Score

I hope I get to go here some day. Maybe I can meet one of the boys that discovered this place. Then I can tell them how much I know about them. I hope they are still alive.

tomorrow and really explore."

So the next day, the boys returned to their secret place. This time they found a gallery leading off the main chamber and a shaft. The walls of both were covered with paintings.

Later that day, the boys decided to tell Monsieur Laval, their school teacher, about their great find. He realized at once that, if the boys' story were true, they had stumbled upon what might be one of the most important sites of prehistoric paintings ever discovered. But he decided to go and look for himself, just to make sure before telling everyone else.

Six days later, after the boys had cleared and widened the hole still further, the schoolmaster entered the cave. As soon as he saw the paintings he knew the boys had been right. This was an extraordinary find.

The news of Lascaux Cave spread fast. Soon historians and tourists were flocking to Montignac to see the paintings. Today the ancient paintings have begun to suffer from exposure to the air, so the climate in the cave is carefully controlled. Scientists and historians are at work there, trying to find out more about the paintings and the people who painted them.

If you are ever lucky enough to be shown around Lascaux Cave, your guide could be none other than Jacques Marsal, one of the boys who first stumbled on the hole between the roots of a dead tree all those years ago!

Jenny Wood. *"An Amazing Discovery," Caves: Facts, Stories, Projects.* New York: Two-Can Publishing Ltd, 1990, pp. 1–10.

Student B
Middle Score

It would be totally neat to find a big cave and I think the boys should explore everything in it and mak something out of it, It sure would be neat.

Student C
Low Score

Introduction to Students A, B, and C

You have examined the margin responses of Student A (high), Student B (middle), and Student C (low). Now you are going to examine the response of each student to eight questions about the informational text.

The outstanding (high) responses of Student A were judged using the following rubric. This rubric is a rewrite of a California rubric and includes the four domains of knowledge. Scores are based on the margin notes that appear in the left-hand column that runs alongside the story, as well as the responses to questions 1–8 which follow. A summary commentary appears at the end of the student responses.

H i g h   R u b r i c

Cognition: Readers are fluent, able to process print with ease. These good readers take risks. They entertain challenging ideas and explore multiple possibilities of meaning as they read, grounding these meanings in their acute perceptions of textual and cultural complexities. They often revise their understanding of a text as they reread and as additional information or insight becomes available to them. They fill in gaps in a text, making warranted and responsible assumptions about unstated causes or motivations, or drawing meaning from subtle cues. They are able to change their minds and to articulate a newly developed level of understanding.

Rhetoric: Readers challenge the text. They carry on a dialogue with the writer, raising questions, taking exception, agreeing or disagreeing, appreciating or criticizing text features. They may sometimes suggest ways of rewriting the text. They may test the validity of the author's ideas or information by considering the authority of the author and the nature and quality of evidence presented. They may speculate about the ideological or cultural or historical biases that may inform a text, sometimes recognizing and embracing and sometimes resisting the position that a text seems to construct for its reader. NOTE: Some reading teachers may find it strange to call the reader-text relationship a rhetorical relationship. We ask you to give the notion some consideration.

Linguistics/Conventions: The reader has excellent command of the basics (phonemic awareness, sentence sense). An exemplary reading performance is insightful, discerning, and perceptive as the reader constructs and reflects on structures in a text. Readers at this level are sensitive to linguistic nuances and complexities. They differentiate between literal and figurative meanings, and they recognize how the overall text is structured.

Themes/Ideas: Readers develop connections with and among texts. They recognize real or seeming contradictions, exploring possibilities for their resolution or tolerating ambiguities. Students demonstrate their understanding of the whole work as well as an awareness of how the parts work together to create the whole. They connect their understanding of the text not only to their own ideas, experience, and knowledge, but to their history as participants in a culture or larger community, often making connections to other texts or other works of art. Exceptional readers draw on evidence from the text to generate, validate, expand, and reflect on their own ideas. Good readers recognize that information and ideas are basic building blocks of meaning.

1. **What are your thoughts and feelings about what you have read? Take a few moments to write your response.**

I think this story would be good in a tourist manual because I'm sure many people that go to France would like to go to Lascaux Cave. I would like to go to Lascaux Cave myself so I can meet the real boys, Marcel, Simon, Georges, and Jacques, and tell them that I read a story about them and their amazing discovery.

I wonder if me and my friends would once discover a wonderful thing and get rich and famous. Then Jenny Wood could write a story about me and my friends and the wonderful discovery we discovered.

Student A

2. Draw a picture about the "amazing discovery" described in this selection.

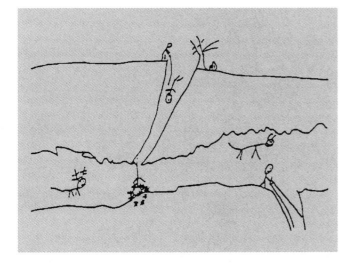

3. Explain your picture.

Marcel found a deep hole near a dead tree. They came back another day with rope and a lamp. They went down the hole and saw dots and lines on the wall. But they turned out to be paintings.

4. Think of some questions you would like to ask Marcel, Jacques, Georges, and Simon about their discovery. Write your questions on the lines below.

Did it hurt when you fell through the hole?
How big was the whole chamber?

How many paintings were there?
Was the cave very spooky?

5. What did you learn from the experience of these explorers? Give examples.

Just because your young, doesn't mean you can't be an explorer I learned that no matter what the problem or situation you are in, you should always be brave. Like when the four boys were exploring the cave, they were brave. They also used their ingenuity.

Student A — High

6. Look at the two pictures below. Circle the picture that you think would be better to use with the story you just read.

7. Tell why you think the picture you circled would be the better choice.

The story wasn't about a caveman painting the walls, it was about four friends that discovered a secret cave and explored it. It did mention cavemen, but it wasn't all about cavemen, it was about four kids that discovered caveman paintings.

8. This is your chance to tell anything else you want about the story—what it means to you, what it reminds you of, how it relates to your own life, or whatever else you think is important.

I have had a great discovery before. It was a surprise birthday party for me.

Before my birthday, my family was acting very strange. They kept whispering to each other. But when I asked what was going on, they just said "nothing."

On the day of my birthday, I came home and I heard a word, "surprise." I discovered that my family was setting up a party for me all along. All my relatives were there and some of my friends, too. I discovered that I was having a surprise birthday party.

Commentary for High Exemplar

Readers demonstrating high performance frequently enter into dialogue both with the text and with the author. This paper shows a student who enters immediately into the story by expressing an opinion and posing possibilities about "what might happen if. . . ." In these rich margin-notes, the student continues to record questions and express opinions about the boys and their actions. We can follow this reader's thinking as he reacts to passages he has marked ("Do you mean they go to the same house for dinner?"). The reader fills in the gaps in light of his knowledge of human nature, concluding that "Simon is the smart one and Marcel is the spirited one." He draws conclusions from the evidence in the story, as in the comment that "I don't think they are professional explorers . . . they should tell someone because what if they get trapped or killed. . . ." In his drawing and comments, the reader reflects some overall comprehension of the facts of the story. This reader can distance himself from the text, posing possibilities and indicating his sense of learning: "Maybe I can meet one of the boys. . . . Then I can tell them how much I know about them."

The reader knows that this story is "about four kids that discovered caveman paintings" (response to question 7), but he rethinks these facts. The story of this discovery he notes, "would be good in a tourist manual." The consequence of the boys' fame might be that he "can meet the real boys." Further, he knows that the significance of a famous find is that you "get rich and famous" and then authors like "Jenny Wood could write a story . . ." (response to question 1).

Readers at a high performance level are able to rethink the meaning of a text, seeing in it a more universal significance. "Just because your young," states this reader, "doesn't mean you can't be an explorer." He recognizes the courage and "ingenuety" of the four boys and understands "that no matter what the problem or situation you are in, you should always be brave."

This paper demonstrates, in a discerning and insightful reading, an understanding of the whole work as well as the ability to participate vicariously in the experience of the boys in the story. Although many high papers will cluster their strengths in a few of the questions, this reader uses every opportunity to continue his reflective reading. As you look carefully at this paper, remember that you are reading the responses that a fourth-grade student was able to write down within the time constraints of one classroom period. It is an impressive performance.

Student B   Middle

The responses of Student B were judged using the following rubric for middle readers. The score was based on the margin notes that appear in the right-hand column that runs alongside the story, as well as the responses to questions 1–8, which follow. A summary commentary appears at the end of the student responses.

Middle Rubric

Cognition: Readers process print fluently. While confident, they rarely take risks. They accept the text without exploring multiple possibilities of meaning. They tend to present their understanding of a text as fixed and rarely revise their interpretation as they reread and as additional information becomes available. These readers have command of many basic reading strategies. They fill in some gaps in a text, making assumptions about unstated causes or motivations or drawing meaning from cues in the text.

Rhetoric: Readers sometimes challenge or question the text. They may raise questions and may agree or disagree without explaining their reactions. They usually differentiate between literal and figurative meanings. They may recognize real or seeming contradictions, but are sometimes distracted by these contradictions and by ambiguities. They demonstrate a thoughtful understanding of the whole work.

Linguistics/Conventions: The reader has a good phonemic awareness and sentence sense.

Themes/Ideas: Readers develop connections with and among texts. They usually connect their understanding of the text to their own experience and knowledge and sometimes to other texts. When directed, these readers may generate, validate, expand, and/or reflect on their ideas about the text, but with less depth. These readers tend to paraphrase or retell, often thoroughly and purposefully. They also see, however, a more general significance in or wider application of the literal facts of the text. They present a plausible and sometimes thoughtful interpretation.

---

1. **What are your thoughts and feelings about what you have read? Take a few minutes to write your response.**

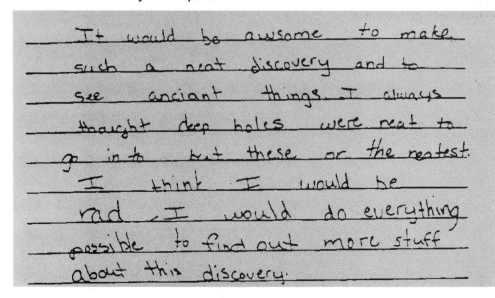

It would be awsome to make such a neat discovery and to see anciant things. I always thought deep holes were neat to go into but these or the neatest. I think I would be rad. I would do everything possible to find out more stuff about this discovery.

2. Draw a picture about the "amazing discovery" described in this selection.

3. Explain your picture.

It is one of the boys coming out
of the whole and seeing the
painting of the prehistoric paintings.

4. Think of some questions you would like to ask Marcel, Jacques, Georges, and Simon about their discovery. Write your questions on the lines below.

How did you find the hole?

What did you do when
you were in the hole?
What were your feelings when
you went in?
Why did you tell your teacher
about the hole?

5. What did you learn from the experience of these explorers? Give examples.

I learned that you should
learn to explore stuff and find
more about the unknown.
I learned you should try more
things from stuff you don't know about

Student B

Middle

6. Look at the two pictures below. Circle the picture that you think would be better to use with the story you just read.

7. Tell why you think the picture you circled would be the better choice.

In the story It didn't say
cavemen were in it carving
paintings. The story didn't say
the boys saw or met an
old man carving things.

8. This is your chance to tell anything else you want about the story—what it means to you, what it reminds you of, how it relates to your own life, or whatever else you think is important.

It is neat and it should
be told to people and this relates
to me because I like to find stuff
and I like to dig and go down holes
and other old, neat things.
It would be totally neat to
find an old cave and find stuff
I would be jazzed.

Commentary for Middle Exemplar

This reader has constructed a thoughtful and plausible interpretation of the text. In this performance there is evidence of immediate engagement with the text, revealed in the margins as questions and rephrasings that parallel the action of the text, as in, "I'm wondering if they will go down in the hole. I would be scared . . . would want to go in again . . . and keep it a secret. . . . I think the boys should explore everything . . . it sure would be neat." The reader is clearly able to follow the story line of the text and connect this understanding with personal experience and knowledge. In response to question 1, the reader says, "I would do everything possible to find more stuff about this discovery."

The reader knows that the discovery is "of the prehistoric paintings." In response to question 4, however, the reader goes beyond the literal facts of the text when he questions, "What were your feelings when you went in? Why did you tell your teacher about the hole?"

In response to question 5, the reader generalizes: "I learned that you should learn to explore stuff and find more about the unknown. I learned you should try more things from stuff you don't know about." The reader has made an interesting but predictable response without the depth of understanding of Student A's response.

In response to question 8, the reader recounts actions that parallel the story: "I like to find stuff and I like to dig and go down holes. . . . It would be totally neat to find an old cave and find stuff." Although there is evidence that the reader understands the work as a whole, his understanding of the text has remained fixed. He has accepted the text without exploring the possibilities of meaning found in more developed performances.

Student C

The responses of Student C were judged using the following rubric for low readers. Scores are based on the student's responses in margin notes and to questions 1–8, which follow. You will notice that the student did not answer all of the questions. In addition, the student did not make margin notes. A summary commentary appears at the end of the student's responses.

L o w   R u b r i c

Cognition: Readers tend to have some problems processing print. They devote so much attention to turning the code into meaning that they have little time left for interpretations, asking questions, and so forth.

Rhetoric: Readers seldom ask questions of a text or offer meaningful evaluations of what they read. They tend to abandon sections of text or become entangled in difficult sections of a text.

Linguistics/Conventions: Readers have some basic sense of sentence structure and conventions, but tend to be vague about parts of overall text structure.

Themes/Ideas: A limited reading performance indicates that readers construct partial and/or reductive meanings for a text. They may demonstrate a superficial understanding of parts of the text. They demonstrate a reductive meaning for the text by overgeneralizing or oversimplifying but seem unable to grasp the whole. Low readers develop few or no connections with texts. They may, as they recognize some idea, continue to write or draw, but their responses will appear to have only a tangential relevance to the text.

---

1. **What are your thoughts and feelings about what you have read? Take a few minutes to write your response.**

> I think my feelings and thougts are that Marcel shouted to his friends because there was a dead tree And then Jaques seen a strange hole under the tree and that hole did seem to have no end And it was dark in the hole.

Student C

Low

2. Draw a picture about the "amazing discovery" described in this selection.

4. Think of some questions you would like to ask Marcel, Jacques, Georges, and Simon about their discovery. Write your questions on the lines below.

Macel why was there a hole
under the dead tree.
Jaques where you scared
when you went in the hole
Georges did you found eneything
down that hole.
Simon would you tell
someone about what yo found

3. Explain your picture.

I did when Marcel isshouting
to his friends to come and
see what he found and it was
a dead tree and then theyseen
a strange houle under the tree and
the went in there it was dark

5. What did you learn from the experience of these explorers? Give examples.

I learn that the boys where
the first explorers to go down
to the hole.

71

Student C — Low

6. Look at the two pictures below. Circle the picture that you think would be better to use with the story you just read.

8. This is your chance to tell anything else you want about the story—what it means to you, what it reminds you of, how it relates to your own life, or whatever else you think is important.

this means to me is that why was a the tree dead. It reminds me of going in side in the hole and get allot of gold in the hole.

It relates me why they didn't go to school those days.

7. Tell why you think the picture you circled would be the better choice.

I think the picture I chose was the best because it looks like the hole. And Georges had a oil lamp in his hand.

Low

Student C

Commentary for Low Exemplar

In a low reading performance, readers generally focus on one segment or one idea of the text. Almost every response relates directly to the first few paragraphs of the text. There is some meager evidence of connections to other events in the text "... the boys where the first explorers to go down to the hole," and "Georges had a oil lamp in his hand." But there is no evidence that this reader grasped the gist or "whole" of the text.

This reader would benefit from extended conversations about the texts that she reads, both with her peers and with a teacher who could probe for greater depth of understanding. At this time, however, the reader demonstrates only a partial, limited understanding of this informational text.

Connections to Standards

	STANDARDS											
	1	2	3	4	5	6	7	8	9	10	11	12
Targeted	*1*	*2*	*3*	4	5	*6*	7	8	9	10	11	12
Supplementary	*1*	*2*	*3*	*4*	5	*6*	7	8	*9*	*10*	11	*12*

The targeted standards are 1, 2, 3, and 6. Responses to informational texts require students to apply a range of strategies to comprehend, interpret, evaluate, and critique texts (1, 2, 3, 6). When embedded in classroom instruction, responses might also include visual representations (4) and texts might include such nonprint sources as films, television, and radio broadcasts (1). Depending on the texts being read or viewed and the responses being elicited or offered, responding to informational texts can help students develop an understanding of and respect for diversity (9). Students whose first language is not English can use their first language to develop understanding of texts (10). Students can use responses to informational texts to accomplish their own purposes, such as developing and exploring an interpretation of a self-selected novel (12).

Task

In reading records, fourth-grade students were asked to provide evidence that they had read:
- at least twenty-five books (or their equivalent in articles, newspapers, or textbooks) in the course of a year;
- materials that are age-appropriate and high-quality, e.g., chosen from recognized reading lists;
- a well-balanced selection of materials from *classic and contemporary* literature and from *public discourse* (documentary essays, news analyses, editorials);
- at least *three different kinds (genres)* of printed materials (for example, novels, biographies, magazine articles);
- works of at least five different authors;
- at least *four books (or book equivalents) about one issue,* or in one genre, or by a single author (or a combination of all of these).

Exemplar

Rubric

- The reader appears to meet all of the necessary requirements listed in the task (see above).

- The reader presents a well-documented record of the reading.

- A few of the selections are very short, but most of the selections are adequate or better.

- An evaluation column would improve the record.

- Beginning date of reading (last column) would help the teacher estimate pace.

- Four books on one issue should be marked.

- Genre should be marked.

- Classics should be marked.

Date Begun	Title of the Book	Author's Name	Number of Pages	Date Finished
09/05/95	Garfield, Fat Cat 3 Pack	Jim Davis	480	09/28/95
09/05/95	Q is for Duck	Elting & Folsom	55	09/05/95
09/05/95	A Writer	M.B. Goffstein	26	09/05/95
09/06/95	The Wright Brothers	Quentin Reynolds	183	09/29/95
10/02/95	Old Whirlwind	Elizabeth Coatsworth	62	10/05/95
10/03/95	The Story of Jumping Mouse	John Steptoe	50	10/03/95
10/03/95	The Ghosts	Antonia Barber	214	10/25/96
10/05/95	Accept No Substitutes	Stan & Jan Berenstain	102	10/16/95
10/20/95	Ben Franklin	John Tottle	192	12/10/95
10/26/95	Key to the Treasure	Peggy Parish	154	11/07/96
11/09/95	The Pied Piper of Hamelin	Robert Browning	10	11/09/96
11/13/95	The Cremation of Sam McGee	Robert Service	20	11/13/96
11/14/95	Borrowed Black	Ellen Bryan Obed	40	11/14/96
11/16/95	Henry O. Tanner, Artist	Mildred D. Johnson	4	11/16/96
11/27/95	The Christmas Secret	Joan Lexau	47	11/27/96

continued on page 75

Date Begun	Title of the Book	Author's Name	Number of Pages	Date Finished
11/28/95	The Best Christmas Pageant Ever	Barbara Robinson	80	12/05/96
12/06/95	A Word to the Wise	Alison Cragin Herzig & Jane Lawerence Mali	186	01/09/96
12/11/95	Say Cheese & Die!	R. L. Stine	132	01/05/96
01/10/96	The House on Hackman's Hill (I)	Joan Lowery Nixon	62	01/19/96
01/11/96	Two Minutes Mysteries	Donald J. Sobol	160	01/11/96
01/22/96	The Horror PII	Joan Lowery Nixon	60	01/30/96
01/09/96	The Cuckoo Clock of Doom	R. L. Stine	118	01/28/96
01/29/96	The Haunted Hash	R. L. Stine	128	02/09/96
01/01/96	My Harriest Adventure	R. L. Stine	133	02/20/96
02/05/96	Piano Lessons Can Be Murdur	R. L. Stine	124	02/27/96
02/06/96	Lost on a Mountain in Maine	Donn Kendler	125	02/22/96
02/26/96	The Shadow in the Pond	Ron Roy	91	03/17/96
03/04/96	Babe	Pick King Smith	104	03/06/96
03/01/96	Larry Bird, Drive	Bob Ryan & Larry Bird	290	04/26/96
03/18/96	Summer of the Monkeys	Wilson Rawls	283	
04/27/96	The Curse of the Mummy's Tomb	R. L. Stine	132	
04/29/96	The Great Cheese Conspiracy	Jean Van Leeuwen	92	

Commentary

This fourth grader has documented an impressive amount of reading from September to mid-April for a total of 32 books or book equivalents. The books listed are generally high quality texts. The student has read a well-balanced selection of materials from classic and contemporary literature (e.g., *The Pied Piper of Hamlin, Summer of the Monkeys*). The student has read in a variety of genres, including autobiography, biography, poetry, mystery, and horror fiction. The works of many different authors are represented here. The student has exceeded the depth requirement by reading 6 books by R. L. Stine, as well as several other works in the mystery genre.

Exemplar

Date Begun	Title of the Book	Author's Name	Rating	Genre	Reflection
08/19/94	Boys are Yucko	Anna G. Hines	★★★★★	Realistic Fiction	This is funny
08/23/94	Tales of a 4th Grade Nothing	Judy Blume	★★★★★★	Realistic Fiction	I recomend this to people that laugh
08/24/94	Michael Gets the Measles		★★★★	Realistic Fiction	It is okay
10/03/95	The Story of Jumping Mouse	John Steptoe	★★★★★★	Realistic Fiction	
08/25/94	T.A.A.S. Scott & Coach		★★★★	Realistic Fiction	Good
08/25/94	Election Day	Johanna Hurwitz	★★★★★★	Realistic Fiction	This is funny
08/30/94	Chin Chian & the Dragon Prince		★★★★★★	Folklore	Great
09/01/94	Rattle Your Bones		★★★★★★	How to	Excellent
09/02/94	A Taste of Blackberries	Doris Smith	★★★★★★	Realistic Fiction	Sad
09/08/94	Tales of a 4th Grade Nothing	Judy Blume	★★★★★★	Realistic Fiction	Extremly Funny
09/09/94	United States Book		★★	Informational	Boring
09/12/94	A Taste of Blackberries	Doris Smith	★★★★★★	Realistic Fiction	Sad
09/13/94	A Taste of Blackberries	Doris Smith	★★★★★★	Realistic Fiction	Sad
09/14/94	A Taste of Blackberries	Doris Smith	★★★★★★	Realistic Fiction	Sad
09/14/94	Magic School Bus / Human Body		★★★★★★	Fiction	Great
09/16/94	Black Widows	Loise Martin	★★★★★★	Informational	Scary
09/17/94	A Taste of Blackberries	Doris Smith	★★★★★★	Realistic Fiction	Sad
09/18/94	The Gold Coin	Alma Ada	★★★★★★	Folklore	Great
09/18/94	A Taste of Blackberries	Doris Smith	★★★★★★	Realistic Fiction	Sad
09/20/94	An Evening Alone		★★★★★	Realistic Fiction	Okay
09/21/94	A Taste of Blackberries	Doris Smith	★★★★★★	Realistic Fiction	Sad
09/21/94	The Gold Coin	Alma Ada	★★★★★★	Folklore	Great
09/22/94	Davis Family		★★★★★★	Fiction	Okay
09/26/94	Music, Music, for Everyone	Vera B. Williams	★★★★★★	Realistic Fiction	Helpful
09/27/94	The Grouchy Ladybug	Eric Carle	★★★★★★	Fiction	Funny
10/17/94	The Great Kapok		★★★★★★	Fantasy	Cool
10/17/94	Scariest Stories You Ever Heard		★★★★★★	Fantasy	Scary
10/17/94	Smoke Free Class of 2003		★★★★★★	Informational	Live
10/18/94	The Ghosts of War	Daniel Cohen	★★★★★★	Folklore	Scary
10/18/94	T.A.S.S. Insects		★★★★★★	Informational	O.K.
10/19/94	True Story of the 3 Little Pigs	Jon Sciezka	★★★★★★	Fantasy	Cool

continued on page 77

R u b r i c

- The reader meets all of the necessary requirements listed in the task.
- Length of book (page numbers) would strengthen record.
- Classics should be marked.
- Some authors missing.
- Ratings are excellent.
- Beginning and ending dates of reading needed.
- Genre is marked, but categories need work.
- Four books on one issue should be marked.

Date Begun	Title of the Book	Author's Name	Rating	Genre	Reflection
10/20/94	Sideway Stories		★★★★★★	Fantasy	Great
10/21/94	Sideway Stories		★★★★★★	Fantasy	Awsome
10/24/94	Sideway Stories		★★★★★★	Fantasy	Funny
10/25/95	Sideway Stories		★★★★★★	Fantasy	Cool
10/26/94	Sideway Stories		★★★★★★	Fantasy	Exellent
10/31/94	Halloween Fun		★★★★★★	Puzzle	Exellent
11/01/94	Sideway Stories		★★★★★	Fantasy	Exillerating
11/01/94	Scholastic News		★★★★★★	Informational	Cool
11/02/94	Wayside Stories		★★★★★★	Fantasy	Great
11/02/94	Wayside Stories		★★★★★★	Fantasy	Great
11/02/94	Cougars		★★★★★★	Informational	Cool
11/07/94	Wild Animals		★★★★★★	Informational	Scary
11/07/94	Stormy Rescue		★★★★★★	Fantasy	Excellent
11/07/94	Stormy Rescue		★★★★★★	Fantasy	Radical
11/08/94	Midnight Fright		★★★★★★	Mystery	Estatic
11/08/94	Still More Scary		★★★★★★	Mystery	Scary
11/08/94	Stories for Sleepovers			Mystery	Mysterious
11/08/94	Horror at the Haunted House		★★★★★★	Mystery	Mysterious
11/09/94	Midnight Fright		★★★★★★	Mystery	Cool
11/09/94	Scariest Stories You Ever Heard		★★★★★	Mystery	Great
11/09/94	Horror at the Haunted House		★★★★★★	Mystery	Creepy
11/10/94	Cougars		★★★★★★	Informational	Cool
01/10/95	Our Teacher is Missing	Mary Frances Shura	★★★	Realistic Fiction	1st Chapter is not so funny
01/10/95	T.A.A.S.		★★★★★	Realistic Fiction	Okay
01/10/95	Ship Wrecked on Padre Island	Isabel R. Martin	★★★★	Realistic Fiction	Chapter 2 is not very good
01/11/95	Prize Winning Science Fair Projects		★★★	Information	Not Bad
01/11/95	Foolish Machinery		★★★★★★	Informative	Great
01/11/95	T.A.A.S.		★	Realistic Fiction	Boring
01/12/95	Our Teacher is Missing	Mary Frances Shura	★★★★	Realistic Fiction	2nd Chapter is okay
01/12/95	Ship Wrecked on Padre Island	Isabel R. Martin	★★★★★	Realistic Fiction	3rd Chapter okay
01/13/95	Ship Wrecked on Padre Island	Isabel R. Martin	★★★★★★	Realistic Fiction	4th Chapter is GREAT
01/17/95	Our Teacher is Missing	Mary Frances Shura	★★★★	Realistic Fiction	3rd Chapter is boring

continued on page 78

Date Begun	Title of the Book	Author's Name	Rating	Genre	Reflection
01/17/95	Ship Wrecked on Padre Island	Isabel R. Martin	★ ★ ★ ★ ★ ★	Realistic Fiction	5th Chapter EXCELLENT
01/18/95	Ship Wrecked on Padre Island	Isabel R. Martin	★ ★ ★ ★ ★ ★	Realistic Fiction	6th Chapter EXCELLENT
01/18/95	Ship Wrecked on Padre Island	Isabel R. Martin	★ ★ ★ ★ ★ ★	Realistic Fiction	7th Chapter is EXCELLENT
01/23/95	Our Teacher is Missing	Mary Frances Shura	★ ★ ★ ★ ★	Realistic Fiction	4th Chapter is pretty Good
03/02/95	Social Studies		★ ★ ★	Informational	Okay
03/03/95	Big Foot		★ ★	Fantasy	It is a little bit too boring
03/06/95	My Teacher is Missing		★	Realistic Fiction	It was so dumb. It did not have a point.
03/07/95	Tall Tales	Unonamous	★ ★ ★ ★	Folklore	It's okay
03/08/95	Ship Wrecked	Isabel Martin	★ ★ ★ ★ ★ ★	Folklore	It has action and adventure
03/09/95	The Story of Texas		★ ★	Informational	I did not like it that much
03/10/95	The Armadillo from Amarillo	Lyne Cherry	★ ★ ★ ★ ★	Fantasy	GREAT
03/20/95	Popcorn Book		★ ★	Fantasy	Too Short
03/20/95	Stephanie in Full House		★ ★ ★	Informational	Not that hot
03/21/95	Rainforest		★ ★ ★ ★ ★ ★	Realistic Fiction	Excellent
03/23/95	Scholastic News	Unknown	★ ★ ★ ★ ★ ★	Informational	It was a great paper
03/27/95	Journey to America	Sonia Levitin	★ ★ ★ ★ ★	Realistic Fiction	Sad yet heart warming
03/28/95	Journey to America	Sonia Levitin	★ ★ ★ ★ ★ ★	Realistic Fiction	Heartwarming with a touch of sadness
03/29/95	Journey to America	Sonia Levitin	★ ★ ★ ★ ★ ★	Realistic Fiction	It is a touch to the heart
04/03/95	Sussana of the Alamo		★ ★ ★ ★	Historical	Rich Heritage Facts
04/04/95	Magic School Bus	Johanna	★ ★ ★ ★ ★	Informational	PRETTY GOOD
04/05/95	Best 20th Century Ghost Stories	David Knight	★ ★ ★ ★ ★ ★	Mystery	Chills my BONES
04/06/95	Olga Dapolga		★	Fantasy	It is Boring and Short
04/07/95	Stories that Must Not Die		★ ★ ★ ★ ★ ★	Historical	Now here's something that will keep you up
04/10/95	Garfield's Ghost Stories		★ ★	Fantasy	Not a bit close to CREEPY!!
04/11/95	World of Music		★ ★ ★ ★ ★	Music	Musical
04/12/95	My Teacher is an Alien		★ ★ ★ ★ ★	Science Fiction	SPOOKY
04/13/95	S. S. Indians		★ ★ ★	Informational	OKAY
04/15/95	Stories that Must Not Die		★ ★ ★ ★ ★ ★	Science Fiction	Super Kaduper SCARY
04/18/95	Magic School Bus—Inside the Earth	Johanna	★ ★ ★ ★ ★	Informational	I can DIG It.
04/18/95	Enchantress from the Stars		★ ★ ★ ★ ★ ★	Fantasy	Out of this world
04/19/95	Enchantress from the Stars		★ ★ ★ ★ ★	Fantasy	Great resemblance to "The Neverending Story"
04/21/95	Creatures from UFO's		★ ★ ★ ★ ★ ★	Science Fiction	It's a saucer of fun.

Commentary

This fourth grader has documented a prodigious amount of reading from August to April—approximately 62 books or book equivalents. The books listed are high quality and age appropriate. The student has read a well-balanced selection of literary and informational texts, including age-appropriate news articles. The student has documented reading in a wide range of genres and authors. The student has read in depth in the areas of realistic fiction and fantasy. The student has used a rating system and comments to indicate engagement with reading. Over the course of the year, the comments developed from simple, one-word reactions to more sophisticated reflections (e.g., "Heartwarming with a touch of sadness"). The final comments suggest a reader who enjoys playing with language (e.g., "I can DIG it." "It's a saucer of fun").

Date Begun	Title of the Book	Author's Name
1	Number the Stars	Lois Lowry
2	Devils Brige	Cynthia DeFelice
3	Black Beuty	Anna Sewell
4	The New Coach	Elizabeth Levy
5	The Gold Cadillac	Michael Hays
6	Treasures Island	Robert Louns
7	My Sister the Trador	Candice F.
8	Lives of the Musicans	Katheleen Kall
9	The Lady Who Put Salt in Her Cofee	Story Works
10	Bill Picket	Sily Humcock
11	April Fools Day	Emily Kelley
12	Sharah Plain and Tall	
13	Dear Diary	Carrie Rundall
14	Almost Famous	Daived Gety
15	Cowboy Country	Dann Herber Scott
16	The Grand Escape	Phyllis Reymols
17	Baby	Ratricia Maclachala
	Charlotts Web	E.B. White

Rubric

The reader falls below the requirements for high achievement, listed in the task requirements. Middle readers tend to read ten to fifteen books and to limit the range (genre, literary, and nonliterary).

Commentary

This fourth grader has documented a moderate amount of reading. Rather than listing dates in the left-hand column, the student has numbered the books. The books are high quality, including works of classic and contemporary literature. The student has read primarily fiction. There is no evidence that the student has read in depth in a particular area. The student has read works of at least five different authors. Genre requirement may not have been met.

Connections to Standards

	STANDARDS											
Targeted	1	2	3	4	5	6	7	8	9	10	11	12
Supplementary	1	2	3	4	5	6	7	8	9	10	11	12

The breadth of reading requirement challenges the student to apply a range of reading strategies for comprehending, interpreting, evaluating, and critiquing texts. The targeted standards are 1, 2, 3, and 6.

Task

Students were asked to prepare a visual representation of books they have read or books they may write. In this task, teachers stressed the importance of the distinction between representation and illustration. The following samples illustrate the features the teachers emphasized.

Exemplar — High

Rubric

Visual Conventions: High quality performance in visual representation includes a good understanding of basic graphics and an inventive and often complicated approach to visualizing ideas.

Commentary

The top graphic is a visual representation of *Charlotte's Web* and the bottom graphic is a visual representation of *Grandpa's Life*. In the graphic for *Charlotte's Web,* crossing lines connect the corners representing characters (Wilber and Templeton, Fern and Charlotte). The side lines appear to show different character relationships. The two sets of parallel vertical lines appear to contrast "love" and "likes" with "doesn't like" and "doesn't really notice." The crossing lines represent "thinks," as do the bottom lines. This is a sophisticated effort which goes a bit astray in its symmetry.

The bottom graphic uses the golf course design to represent *Grandpa's Life.* A number of graphic conventions are used to represent the life. First, birth (Event 1) is set apart, and there is a space between first grade (Event 2) and junior high school (Event 3). Space here represents time. There also appear to be difficult times in life, represented by the right turn in the course (Event 25) and the sand trap (Event 28). Again, this is a sophisticated effort. Both students understand how to use visual conventions.

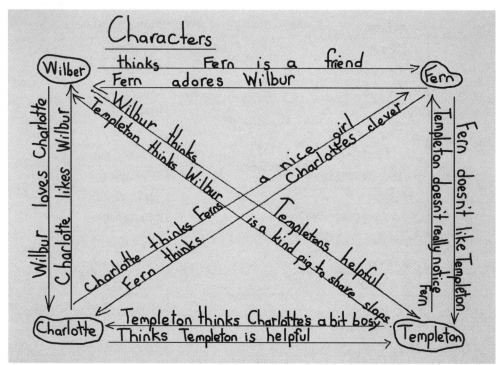

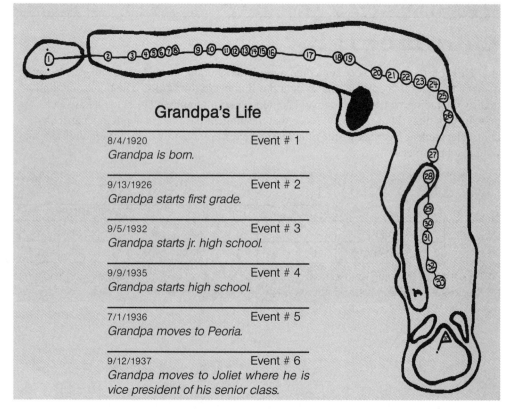

8/4/1920	Event # 1
Grandpa is born.	
9/13/1926	Event # 2
Grandpa starts first grade.	
9/5/1932	Event # 3
Grandpa starts jr. high school.	
9/9/1935	Event # 4
Grandpa starts high school.	
7/1/1936	Event # 5
Grandpa moves to Peoria.	
9/12/1937	Event # 6
Grandpa moves to Joliet where he is vice president of his senior class.	

Middle

Exemplar

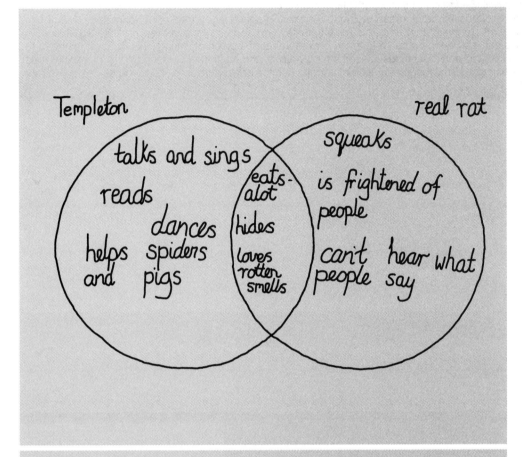

Templeton — talks and sings / reads / dances / helps spiders and pigs — eats alot / hides / loves rotten smells — squeaks / is frightened of people / can't hear what people say — real rat

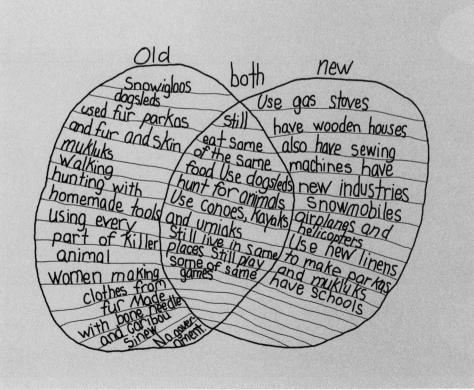

Old — Snowigloos / dogsleds / used fur parkas and fur and skin / mukluks / walking / hunting with homemade tools using every part of killer animal / women making clothes from fur made with bone needle and caribou sinew. No goverment. — both — still eat some of the same food / Use dogsleds / hunt for animals / Use conoes, kayaks and umiaks / Still live in same places / Still play some of same games — new — Use gas stoves / have wooden houses / also have sewing machines / have new industries / Snowmobiles / airplanes and helicopters / Use new linens to make parkas and mukluks / have schools

Commentary

Both students use Venn diagrams correctly (comparison, contrast), but the students need to make a few improvements. The top Venn diagram, which is a representation based on *Charlotte's Web,* needs development. The differences between *Real Rat* and *Templeton* are clear and the similarities are also clear, but more details about differences and similarities would have improved this graphic.

The bottom graphic has substantial detail, but the student tried to push too much into a small space. The Venn diagram needs to be bigger, allowing more room for details. In addition, the student might be able to drop some words like "and" by using graphic conventions—for example, a plus (+) or a comma (,).

These two performances show a middle range in which the basics are under control. However, complexity and inventiveness are missing.

81

Connections to Standards

	STANDARDS											
Targeted	1	2	3	4	5	6	7	8	9	10	11	12
Supplementary	1	2	3	4	5	6	7	8	9	10	11	12

The targeted standard is the use of visual language to communicate effectively with a variety of audiences and for different purposes (4). Visual representation offers students a variety of possibilities for responding to literary and nonliterary, print and nonprint texts (1, 2). It can become a strategy for comprehending, interpreting, evaluating, and appreciating texts (3). In additon, visual representations, such as concept maps, Venn diagrams, and illustrations can play an important role in the development of a piece of writing (4, 5, 6). Students need to refine the distinction among different visual systems and the various uses of charts, graphs, and multimedia presentations for creating and communicating knowledge (7, 8). Students can use visual respresentation to accomplish their own purposes (12), such as designing brochures and enhancing oral presentations.

The section that follows contains excerpts from the portfolios of three elementary school students—Nathan, Mandy, and Daniel. From each portfolio we have selected only a few pieces for inclusion here. In some cases, we show only excerpts of pieces, but enough to give you a general idea of the quality of the whole piece. The purpose of this section is to give you an idea of what a collection of a student's work—as opposed to a single sample—may reveal about that student's learning and accomplishments in English language arts.

The selections from Nathan's, Mandy's, and Daniel's portfolios represent a range of levels of performance—high (Nathan), middle (Mandy), and low (Daniel). We are not suggesting that Nathan's work represents the very best that has been or could ever be done. Likewise, we are not suggesting that Daniel's work represents some absolute minimum level. Our intent is to represent some of the range of performances which teachers encounter in today's heterogeneously grouped classes and to represent the judgments which teachers make about the levels of achievement in those performances, using the *Standards for the English Language Arts* (NCTE/IRA).

Nathan, Mandy, and Daniel are students in different classrooms from different parts of the country. When they assembled their portfolios, they were participating in the second year of the field trial of the New Standards English language arts portfolio system,[1] which was at that time managed by the Literacy Unit at NCTE. This system requires students to show examples of their best work and to follow a common "menu" in putting together their portfolios. This menu was based on the NCTE/IRA standards. Among the required items were:

- evidence of reading accomplishment in literature, informational materials, and public discourse;
- evidence of quantity, range, and depth in reading;
- evidence of writing in a variety of genres or modes (e.g., argument or persuasion, narration, report of information);
- evidence of speaking, listening, and viewing;
- an introductory reflective essay describing what the contents of the portfolio suggest about growth in English language arts;
- a table of contents.

Nathan's, Mandy's, and Daniel's portfolios were scored by teachers in their local states and districts, and then sent to a national meeting, where they were scored by teachers from across the country. Many of these portfolios were scored again by NCTE teachers in NCTE's national meetings. Some of these teachers' judgments and comments appear in the rubric-based marginal comments and the summary commentaries at the end of each portfolio. For the sake of simplicity, rubrics and commentaries are combined into one for each entry. The summaries discuss the degree to which the portfolio as a whole represents achievement in the three ways of knowing (i.e., knowing that, knowing how, knowing about), the four domains of English language arts described in the introduction to this book (i.e., cognition, rhetoric, linguistics/conventions, and cultural themes or ideas), and the six activities or forms of representation of English language arts classes (i.e., reading, writing, speaking, listening, viewing, and representing).

Throughout this section, "Connections to Standards," which appear in the margins, show connections between relevant portions of the NCTE/IRA standards and individual entries. These are not the *only* possible connections that could be made between the standards and the portfolio entries; they are, however, particularly salient connections.

The work that you see here will undoubtedly prompt you to ask many questions about the work itself and about the circumstances leading to and surrounding the production of the final portfolio. We hope that you will pursue these questions with your colleagues and that you will understand that we cannot address here all the provocative issues raised when we study, interpret, and evaluate student work.

---

[1] New Standards is a partnership of approximately twenty states and urban districts working to build an assessment system that measures students' progress toward achieving a set of standards (also being developed by New Standards).

Portfolios

Nathan

Mandy

Daniel

84

Nathan's Portfolio

Nathan, who compiled his portfolio at the end of his fifth-grade year, has selected work representing his development over the course of the school year. We have selected only a few pieces for inclusion here. Some of the pieces are excerpts only. Note: The alphabetic letters in the rubrics/commentaries should be matched with the letters in the margins of the student work, thereby showing the location of the features cited.

Task

Following is Nathan's introductory reflective essay, which is written in the form of a letter addressed to the portfolio reader and creates a portrait of Nathan as a reader, writer, and learner. The passages below illustrate some of Nathan's thinking about his own reading, writing, and learning.

Reflective Essay (Letter) — High

Dear Reader,

A. Hello, my name is _____. I am ten years old and I was born on September 14, 1984 in _____. I am in fifth grade. I go to the Intermediate School. My hobbies are skateboarding, soccer and football. I have one sister, she is in the eighth grade. My address is _____

B. I think that my most challenging school activity is writing. It is writing because when I write ideas don't just pop into my head, I have to take the time to think about an idea that fits the topic. I think the easiest school activity is math because I really understand the concepts and I feel that I do well in it.

C. Three of my favorite pieces of writing are Snow, because I feel that I described a cold winter day and the smooth snow on the tree limbs very well, and when I read this poem I can see the picture in my head of a little boy in a wheelchair looking out of his window at the

D. children having fun in the snow. Call It Courage because I worked very hard on it to make it my best piece. I also am proud of my scary poem "Terrible Thoughts."

Rubric / Commentary

A. Engages the reader by direct address and provides relevant background information.
B. Shows awareness of processes and strategies in writing.
C. Reviews writing accomplishments and explains personal criteria for good writing.
D. Provides specific detail to support claims.

Paper continued on page 86

E. Assesses strengths and progress in reading, writing, and speaking.

F. Sets specific goals for improvement.

G. Aware of progress in writing.

H. Understands academic and personal purposes of portfolio.

Connections to Standards

Nathan demonstrates substantial achievement in:

• participating as a knowledgeable, reflective, creative, and critical member of a literacy community (11).

I am proud of this piece because I won first prize, and I love frightening myself when I read it over and over again.

E. I have grown as a reader this year because I have gotten very good grades on my reading comprehension packets and I have read more independent books this year. I have grown as a writer this year because I got a perfect score on the State Writing Test, and I think my ideas have improved. I have grown as a speaker this year because when I need to ask or answer a question I am not shy about it, I go right ahead and ask it or answer it.

F. In the sixth grade I would like to improve on my Science and my Social Studies because I do not feel that I understand the concepts as well as the other three subjects. I also don't get as good grades in these two subjects, so I would like to improve them.

G. My portfolio means so much to me because it shows how my writing has improved, it is an example of different types of writing challenges and styles of my work. It shows all of my effort, and it shows my imagination and how my thinking skills work. I also think it would be a lot of fun to look at my portfolio in a few years to see what kind of a writer

H. I was when I was ten years old and I was in the fifth grade.

Sincerely,

Task

Nathan's entry slip states that the assignment was to make an invention that would solve a problem, then write a script for a commercial, and present it in class. The commercial is a form of persuasion or argument. Following is the script Nathan wrote for a group performance.

Argument

PRODUCT: NOT HOT POTS

INVENTOR:

A. SLOGAN: Your food will cook, your fingers won't

JINGLE: (sung to the tune of "I got the horse right here" from "Guys and Dolls")

B.
We got the pots right here
And it is very clear
That when you touch the rims you sure will cheer
Not Hot!
Not Hot!
These pot rims do not get hot!

C. COMMERCIAL SCRIPT:
Characters:
Narrator:
Mother: Suzanna
Father: Brian
Kid #1:   Jessie
Kid #2:   Samantha

MOTHER: Ouch!

Kid #1:   Mom are you okay?

Kid #2:   Yeah, are you?

MOTHER: I think so, although I burnt my finger pretty badly. (Father walks in).

FATHER: Honey, what's cooking?

MOTHER: My finger!

FATHER: Again? Oh honey, I'm going to go to the store and buy you some of those new pots and pans I've been hearing about.
(Father rushes out)

NARRATOR: Yes, now you can own the new set of pots and pans called Not Hot Pots for only $15.95 plus $1.50 shipping and handling. What makes these pot the best you can own? The edges are made with a special metal that does not get hot in the oven! Forget about buying cooking gloves and pot holders (throws them over his shoulder) because with this product, your fingers will never be burned when you take the pot or pan out of the oven. For roasting, for baking, for pizza remember. . . . . with Not Hot Pots your food will cook, your fingers won't.

EVERYONE SING JINGLE

Rubric / Commentary

A. Intends to capture and keep the attention of the audience.
B. Applies understanding of advertising techniques, i.e., slogans and jingles.
C. Observes the conventions of script writing.

Task

Following are Nathan's "application" for invention license and visual advertisements.

Rubric/Commentary

A. Observes the conventions of a formal document.

B. Makes insightful connections between his writing and visual presentation.

C. Skillfully combines written and visual language.

Connections to Standards

Nathan demonstrates substantial achievement in:

- applying knowledge of media techniques to create print and nonprint texts (6).

A.

Invention: NOT HOT COOKWARE

I have discovered a metal that will make cooking much easier, better, and safer. It is called Averium. Averium prevents cooks from being burned while holding the cookware. The newly invented metal does not get hot.

Bonded to the edges of the aluminum or stainless steel cookie sheets, pots and pans, Averium lets cooks remove cookware from the oven without burning their fingers. The bonded process will be applied at the factory when the product is being manufactured.

WITNESSED on the 27th day
of January 1995 by

_____

SOLE INVENTOR
JANUARY 27, 1995

B.

C.